⟨ WHO SAID THAT? ⟩

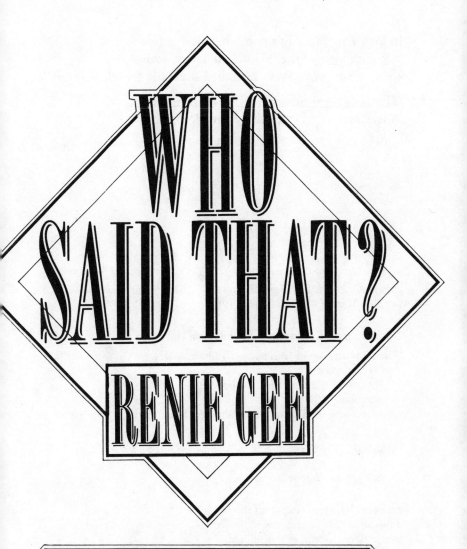

WHO SAID THAT?

RENIE GEE

**Edited and revised by
Graham Donaldson and Maris Ross**

David & Charles
Newton Abbot London

In loving memory of my mother, Renie Gee
(the authoress of the 'Who Said That?' series),
a very courageous lady, who died suddenly on 6th July 1987.

'The Moving Finger writes: and, having writ,
Moves on . . . ' Omar Khayyám, *Rubáiyát*

VALERIE BRIGGS

First published as *Who Said That? (1980)*, *More of Who Said That?* (1981)
and *Still More of Who Said That?* (1983)

British Library Cataloguing in Publication Data

Who said that?: quotations and potted biographies
   of famous people.
   1. Quotations. 2. Persons – Biographies –
   Collections
   I. Gee, Renie II. Donaldson, Graham III Ross, Maris
   080
   ISBN 0-7153-9372-3

Printed in Great Britain
by Billings & Sons Worcester
for David & Charles Publishers plc
Brunel House Newton Abbot Devon

INTRODUCTION

When the late Renie Gee first compiled *Who Said That?*, she described it as a 'fun' book to be looked through with interest and amusement. In the spirit of her original aim, we have revised and expanded the collection of quotes from famous people. We hope you will find in this compilation the wise, the funny, the historic, and some of the most beautiful and moving words in the English language.

The biographies of the people who said these words are equally fascinating, taking us from Confucius in 6th century BC China to Neil Armstrong, the first man on the moon.

As Renie Gee said, if you find your favourite quotation here, that surely is added delight.

GRAHAM DONALDSON, MARIS ROSS

Joseph Addison

What pity is it
That we can die but once to serve our country!

Cato

Thus I live in the world rather as a spectator of mankind than as
one of the species.

In the Spectator

*Joseph Addison (1672–1719) was a British essayist and poet. Born
in Wiltshire, he was granted a pension to enable him to qualify for the
Diplomatic Service by foreign travel, and in 1704 he celebrated Marlborough's victory at Blenheim in his poem* The Campaign. *He became
Under-Secretary of State, Secretary to the Lord Lieutenant of Ireland
and an MP, and founded* The Spectator *in 1711 with his friend Sir
Richard Steele to whose* Tatler *he also contributed.*

Aesop

The gods help them that help themselves.

Fables

It is not only fine feathers that make fine birds.

Fables

Don't count your chickens before they are hatched.

Fables

Familiarity breeds contempt.

The Fox and the Lion

*Aesop (c550BC) was the author of a collection of Greek fables about
animals with human characteristics. Accounts differ of who he was. If
a real person rather than the ancient equivalent of Anonymous, Aesop
came from Phrygia, may have been a slave on Samos, gained his freedom and travelled widely to Babylon and as adviser to Croesus, the
last king of Lydia. He is represented in later art as deformed.*

A Henry Aldrich

If all be true that I do think,
There are five reasons we should drink;
Good wine – a friend – or being dry –
Or lest we should be by and by –
Or any other reason why.

Reasons for Drinking

Henry Aldrich (1647–1710) was an English scholar who became dean of Christ Church, Oxford, in 1689 and remained in office until his death. He designed the Peckwater Quadrangle at Christ Church, adapted anthems and church music, and wrote some humorous verse.

Woody Allen

It's not true that I'm afraid to die, I just don't want to be there when it happens.

Without Feathers, 1976

If only God would give me some clear sign! Like making a large deposit in my name at a Swiss bank.

Woody Allen (1935–), born in Brooklyn, dropped out of college to become a gag writer in his teens and then performed his own jokes as a stand-up comic. He has acted in, written and directed films, including the Oscar-winning Annie Hall *(1977). His special image is the little man overshadowed by his neuroticisms.*

Hans Christian Andersen

His own image. . . was no longer the reflection of a clumsy, dirty, grey bird, ugly and offensive. He himself was a swan.

The Ugly Duckling

'But the Emperor has nothing on at all!' cried a little child.

The Emperor's New Clothes

They could see she was a real princess and no question about it, now that she had felt one pea all the way through twenty mattresses

and twenty more feather beds. Nobody but a princess could be so **A**
delicate.

The Princess and the Pea

Hans Christian Andersen (1805–75) one of the world's greatest story-tellers. The Danish son of a shoemaker, he was born at Odense and his first book was published when he was only seventeen but it was not until 1829 that he attracted notice. In 1835 his novel The Improvisatore *brought him popularity and he began to compose the immortal fairy tales which have since been translated into a great many languages.*

Neil Armstrong

That's one small step for man, one giant leap for mankind.

Spoken 21.7.1969 as first man on moon

Neil Armstrong (1930–), American astronaut born in Ohio, saved his pocket money for flying lessons, going solo before sixteen. He trained in the US Navy as a fighter pilot and was decorated for bravery in the Korean War. After ten years as a civilian test pilot, he was accepted for astronaut training in 1962 and in 1966 made the first docking in outer space. After commanding the moon flight, he made goodwill visits to many countries and taught aerospace engineering for eight years at the University of Cincinnatti.

Matthew Arnold

The sea is calm tonight.
The tide is full, the moon lies fair
Upon the Straits.

Dover Beach

Home of lost causes, and forsaken beliefs, and unpopular names, and impossible loyalties!

'On Oxford' in Essays in Criticism, 1865

Runs it not here, the track by Childsworth Farm,

A Past the high wood, to where the elm-tree crowns
The hill behind whose ridge the sunset flames?

Thyrsis

Once I knew each field, each flower, each stick,
And with the country-folk acquaintance made –

Thyrsis

Matthew Arnold (1822–88), the British poet and son of the famous Doctor Arnold, headmaster of Rugby School, was professor of poetry at Oxford, 1857–67. He wrote a classical tragedy (Merope) *and* New Poems, *and these were followed by his* Essays in Criticism, *some studies in education,* Literature *and* Dogma *and* Culture and Anarchy.

Thomas Arnold

Probably the happiest period in life — middle age.

What we must look for here is, first, religious and moral principles; secondly, gentlemanly conduct; thirdly, intellectual ability.

To pupils at Rugby

Thomas Arnold (1795-1842) was born on the Isle of Wight, and educated at Winchester and Corpus Christi, Oxford, where he gained a first in classics. He was headmaster of Rugby School from 1828 to his death. His principles influenced reforms throughout the English public school system.

Margot Asquith

He has a brilliant mind until he makes it up.

Of Sir Stafford Cripps

Ettie has told enough white lies to ice a cake.

Of Lady Desborough

Lord Birkenhead is very clever, but his brains go to his head.

She's as tough as an ox. She'll be turned into OXO when she dies. **A**
Of a friend

He couldn't see a belt without hitting below it.
Of David Lloyd George

If Kitchener was not a great man, he was, at least, a great poster.

Margot Asquith (1868–1945) was originally Margot Tennant, daughter of Sir Charles Tennant, a rich Glasgow industrialist. In 1894 she married into the famous Asquith family and became known as a celebrated wit, but her volumes of memoirs offended many by their lack of reticence. As wife of the Liberal Prime Minister she had a wide circle of friends and acquaintances.

Jane Austen

Where an opinion is general, it is usually correct.

It is a truth universally acknowledged, that a single man in possession of a good fortune must be in want of a wife.
Pride and Prejudice

One half of the world cannot understand the pleasures of the other.
Emma

Jane Austen (1775–1817) was born at Steventon in Hampshire, where her father was rector. She lived first at her birthplace and later at Bath, Southampton and Chawton. Of her completed novels, Sense and Sensibility *appeared in 1811,* Pride and Prejudice *in 1813,* Mansfield Park *in 1814,* Emma *in December 1815, and* Northanger Abbey *and* Persuasion *posthumously in 1818. She had six brothers and one sister. This family circle, involving her in long visits to relatives, provided her with the material for her novels on middle-class manners.*

B Lauren Bacall

I agree with the Bogart theory that all an actor owes the public is a good performance.

No one has ever written a romance better than we lived it.
By Myself 1978, on her marriage to Bogart

I think your whole life shows in your face and you should be proud of that.

Lauren Bacall (1924–), born in New York, played truant from school to watch Bette Davis films. After Broadway bit parts, she made the cover of Harper's Bazaar in 1943 and was spotted by Hollywood. She starred opposite Humphrey Bogart in To Have and Have Not (1944) and stole not only the film but his heart. They married and appeared in many films together. After Bogart died in 1957, she took a break from film roles but resumed acting in the 1960s and 1970s. Her second marriage to Jason Robards Jr in 1961 ended eight years later in divorce.

Francis Bacon

It is a strange desire men have, to seek power and to lose liberty.

Beauty is like a rich stone, best plain set.

It is natural to die as to be born; and to a little infant, perhaps, the one is as painful as the other.
Essays

God Almighty first planted a garden; and, indeed, it is the purest of human pleasures.
Essays

If the hill will not come to Mahomet, Mahomet will go to the hill.
Essays Of Love

Money is like muck, not good except it be spread. **B**

Essays. Of Seditions and Troubles

The remedy is worse than the disease.

Essays. Of Seditions and Troubles

Francis Bacon (1561–1626) philosopher and statesman, was first Baron Verulam and Viscount St Albans, the younger son of Sir Nicholas Bacon, Lord Keeper in Queen Elizabeth's reign. He went through the various steps of the legal profession and entered Parliament in 1584. He was Lord Chancellor of England 1618–20, but was then briefly imprisoned in the Tower of London for bribe-taking. He used his belief in himself to justify his moral actions, such as taking presents from suitors and prosecuting his friend and patron, the Earl of Essex, for treason.

Hylda Baker

Punctuality is something that if you have it, nobody is ever around to appreciate it.

Hylda Baker (1909–82) was a British comedienne who established herself in northern music-hall tradition and in such films as Saturday Night and Sunday Morning, Up the Junction *and* Nearest and Dearest.

Pierre Balmain

The trick of wearing mink is to look as though you are wearing a cloth coat. The trick of wearing a cloth coat is to look as though you are wearing mink.

Newspaper report

13

B *Pierre Alexandre Balmain (1914–82) was educated at the Lycée de Chambéry and Ecole des Beaux-Arts, Paris. Lack of money forced him to give up studying architecture and he went to work in the Paris fashion world, designing for Molyneux and then Lucien Lelong. He opened his own fashion house in 1945 and designed for the titled and famous in the 1950s.*

Honoré de Balzac

There is no such thing as a great talent without great willpower.

La Muse du Département

Our heart is a treasury; if you spend all its wealth at once you are ruined.

Le Père Goriot, 1835

A good husband is never the first to go to sleep at night or the last to awake in the morning.

Children! You bring them into the world, and they drive you out of it.

The man who can govern a woman can govern a nation.

Laws are spider webs that catch little flies, but cannot hold big ones.

Honoré de Balzac (1799–1850) was the son of the director of the City Hospital at Tours. After studying law he turned to literature, but at first with little success. From 1829 onwards he wrote novels depicting contemporary French society. Although he produced a prodigious eighty-five novels in twenty years, his hard work never rewarded him sufficiently to clear debts from prior business speculations.

J.M. Barrie

The God to whom little boys say their prayers has a face very like their mother's.

It's a sort of bloom on a woman. If you have it [charm] you don't need to have anything else.

What Every Woman Knows

His lordship may compel us to be equal upstairs, but there will **B**
never be equality in the servants' hall.

The Admirable Crichton

When the first baby laughed for the first time, the laugh broke
into a thousand pieces and they all went skipping about, and that
was the beginning of fairies.

Peter Pan, 1904

J.M. Barrie (Sir James Matthew Barrie, 1860–1937) was a Scottish novelist and dramatist. After a spell as a journalist in Nottingham, he settled in London and wrote a series of autobiographical novels. From 1890 he also wrote for the theatre. The works which brought him great success after the turn of the century include Quality Street, The Admirable Crichton, Peter Pan, Dear Brutus *and* Mary Rose.

John Barrymore

The way to fight a woman is with your hat. Grab it and run.
You never realize how short a month is until you pay alimony.

John Barrymore (1882–1942) was a celebrated American stage and screen actor, brother of Ethel and Lionel Barrymore. He was an idol with a great 'profile'. He became famous as a romantic movie star of the twenties and for his Hamlet, but later he squandered his talents in inferior comedies and developed an alcohol problem. His four marriages accounted for his cynicism.

Thomas Haynes Bayly

Absence makes the heart grow fonder,
Isle of Beauty, Fare thee well!

Isle of Beauty

Thomas Haynes Bayly (1797–1839) was an English writer of songs and verse. He was born in Bath and should have followed his father into law but preferred writing humorous articles. His father then encouraged him to study for the church but he also gave that up for lyrical poetry, ballads and pieces for the stage which were very popular in their day.

Max Beerbohm

There is much to be said for failure. It is more interesting than
success.

Mainly on the Air, 1946

B The dullard's envy of brilliant men is always assuaged by the suspicion that they will come to a bad end.

Zuleika Dobson, 1911

Sir Max Beerbohm (1872–1956) English writer and cartoonist, was the half-brother of the actor-manager Sir Herbert Beerbohm-Tree. He contributed to The Yellow Book of Essays *and succeeded Shaw as dramatic critic to the* Saturday Review. *He was knighted in 1939. His exhibitions of caricatures in the 1920s aroused controversy.*

Brendan Behan

We have flower battles just as they do in Nice. Only here we throw the pots as well.

On the Dublin Festival, 10 July, 1960

Brendan Behan (1923–64), Irish author and playwright, was a housepainter by trade. He started writing in 1951, achieving success in 1956 with his play The Quare Fellow *which was based on his own prison experiences. Other works followed, including* Borstal Boy, The Hostage *and* Brendan Behan's Island.

David Bellamy

Take nothing but photographs.
Leave nothing but footprints.

On tourists visiting unspoilt places, 1988

David Bellamy (1933–), the ebullient English botanist and broadcaster, has popularised his field of science through television series like Bellamy's Britain *(1975) and* Botanic Man *(1978). He has written extensively on botanical subjects and is an ardent conservationist.*

Hilaire Belloc

How did the party go in Portland Square?
I cannot tell you: Juliet was not there,

And how did Lady Gaster's party go?
Juliet was next to me, and I do not know.

Blinding Love

I'm tired of Love: I'm still more tired of Rhyme.
But Money gives me pleasure all the time.

Epigrams

I will hold my house in the high wood
Within a walk of the sea,
And the men that were boys when I was a boy
Shall sit and drink with me.

The South Country

Do you remember an inn, Miranda?
Do you remember an inn?
And the tedding and the spreading
Of the straw for a bedding,
And the fleas that tease in the high Pyrenees. . .

Tarantella

The nicest child I ever knew
Was Charles Augustus Fortescue

Cautionary Tales

Joseph Hilaire Pierre Belloc (1870–1953) was the son of a French barrister and an English mother. He founded the Eye-Witness *in collaboration with Cecil Chesterton, with whom he also wrote a political work entitled* The Party System. *He also worked with G.K. Chesterton, and his literary versatility is shown by his nonsense verse, his historical studies of Danton, Robespierre and James II, his* History of England, *and various satires.*

Robert Benchley

Drawing on my fine command of language, I said nothing.

It took me 15 years to discover that I had no talent for writing,

B but I couldn't give it up because by that time I was too famous.

Robert Benchley (1889–1945), the American humorist, was born at Worcester, Mass, went to New York as a journalist and became drama editor of the New Yorker. *His books* Of All Things *and* Benchley Beside Himself *demonstrate his fine ability to extract humour from daily life.*

Edmund Clerihew Bentley

Sir Christopher Wren
Said, 'I am going to dine with some men.
If anyone calls
Tell them I'm designing St. Paul's.'

The art of Biography
Is different from Geography.
Geography is about maps,
But Biography is about chaps.

What I like about Clive
Is that he is no longer alive.
There is a great deal to be said
For being dead.

Biography for Beginners

Edmund Clerihew Bentley (1875–1956) was a journalist and novelist whose detective story, Trent's Last Case, *transformed the genre from the Conan Doyle mould to modern realism. He invented the 'clerihew', an epigrammatic verse-form consisting of two rhymed couplets, usually dealing with the character or career of a well-known person.*

Irving Berlin

We depend largely on tricks, we writers of songs. There is no such thing as a new melody.

The toughest thing about success is that you've got to keep on **B**
being a success.

Irving Berlin (1888–), the American song writer, was born in Russia
as Israel Baline. He settled in New York in 1893 near Tin Pan Alley
and wrote 15,000 songs under the name bequeathed him by a printer's
error, Irving Berlin. His centenary in 1988 was spent in the privacy
of his Manhattan home while radio stations played his evergreen hits
like God Bless America, White Christmas, Alexander's Ragtime
Band, Always *and* Annie Get Your Gun.

Josh Billings

It is the little bits of things that fret and worry us; we can dodge
an elephant, but we can't dodge a fly.

Consider the postage stamp; its usefulness consists in the ability
to stick to one thing till it gets there.

There is one kind of laugh that I always recommend; it looks out
of the eye first with a merry twinkle, then it creeps down on to its
hands and knees and plays around the mouth like a pretty moth
around the haze of a candle.

A dog is the only thing on earth that loves you more than you
love yourself.

Silence is one of the hardest arguments to refute.

My advice to those who are about to begin, in earnest, the journey
of life, is to take their heart in one hand and a club in the other.
The Complete Works of Josh Billings

Josh Billings (1818–85) was the pseudonym of Henry Wheeler Shaw,
an American humorous writer. His popular work Josh Billings, His
Sayings *depended for its humour on deliberate mis-spellings, puns and*
malapropisms.

Laurence Binyon

They shall not grow old, as we that are left grow old;
Age shall not weary them, nor the years condemn.

B At the going down of the sun, and in the morning,
We will remember them.

For the Fallen

*Laurence Binyon (1869–1943) poet and art historian, was born in
Lancaster, the son of a clergyman, and became Keeper of Prints and
Drawings at the British Museum. He published some studies of Eng-
lish and Eastern art, but is best remembered for his fine ode* For the
Fallen, *which was written in 1914. It is said and sung at memorial
services and inscribed on many war memorials.*

William Blake

Tyger! Tyger! burning bright
In the forests of the night,
What immortal hand or eye
Could frame thy fearful symmetry?

Songs of Experience: The Tyger

Bring me my bow of burning gold!
Bring me my arrows of desire!
Bring me my spear! O clouds, unfold!
Bring me my chariot of fire.

I will not cease from mental fight,
Nor shall my sword sleep in my hand,
Till we have built Jerusalem
In England's green and pleasant land.

Milton, Preface

To see a World in a Grain of Sand,
And a Heaven in a Wild Flower –
Hold Infinity in the palm of your hand,
And Eternity in an hour.

Auguries of Innocence

A robin redbreast in a cage
Puts all Heaven in a rage.

Auguries of Innocence

O Rose, thou art sick!
The invisible worm
That flies in the night,
In the howling storm,
Has found out thy bed
Of crimson joy,
And his dark secret love
Does thy life destroy.

The Sick Rose

William Blake (1757–1827), English poet, artist and mystic, was apprenticed to an engraver and studied at the Academy under Reynolds. He engraved the illustrations for his Book of Thel, Marriage of Heaven and Hell *and* Song of Los, *but after the failure of an exhibition in 1809 he retired from engraving. His works include* Milton, Jerusalam *and the fragmentary* Everlasting Gospel. *He believed his work was guided by visitations from the spiritual world.*

Humphrey Bogart

Here's looking at you, kid.

As Rick in Casablanca, 1943

Play it, Sam. Play 'As Time Goes By'.

As Rick in Casablanca

Humphrey Bogart (1899–1957), the memorable American film actor, was born in New York, the son of a doctor. He served in the US Navy in World War I. From managing a touring company, he took to the stage and then lone wolf screen roles, including The African Queen, The Maltese Falcon *and* Casablanca. *Many of his films were with his fourth wife, Lauren Bacall, whom he married in 1945. She lost him to cancer.*

James Boswell

I shall never forget the indulgence with which he (Samuel Johnson) treated Hodge, his cat, for whom he himself used to go out and buy oysters, lest the servant having that trouble should take a dislike to the poor creature.

The Life of Samuel Johnson, Hodge the Cat

B   He who praises everybody praises nobody.

The Life of Samuel Johnson

A man, indeed, is not genteel when he gets drunk; but most vices may be committed very genteelly. A man may debauch his friend's wife genteelly; he may cheat at cards genteelly.

The Life of Samuel Johnson

James Boswell (1740–95) was a Scottish biographer and man of letters. He studied law but centred his ambition on literature and politics. He is most famous for his biography, The Life of Samuel Johnson. *Their first meeting was in 1763, and this was followed in 1764 with the formation of the Literary Club, the original members of which included Reynolds, Burke and Goldsmith. Garrick and C.J. Fox joined soon after, and it was here that Boswell became so closely associated with Johnson and took great interest in the formation of his* Dictionary *(published in 1755).*

Rupert Brooke

If I should die, think only this of me:
That there's some corner of a foreign field
That is for ever England.

The Soldier

Stands the Church clock at ten to three?
And is there honey still for tea?

The Old Vicarage:
Grantchester

God! I will pack, and take a train,
And get me to England once again!
For England's the one land, I know,
Where men with splendid hearts may go;
And Cambridgeshire, of all England,
The shire for men who understand;

And of *that* district I prefer
The lovely hamlet, Grantchester.

*The Old Vicarage
Grantchester*

Rupert Chawner Brooke (1887–1915) best known of the English war poets, was the son of a master at Rugby, where he was educated before going to King's College, Cambridge. His first volume of verse was published in 1911. With the outbreak of war in 1914 he took part in the unsuccessful defence of Antwerp, and early in 1915 he was sent to the Mediterranean, where he died of dysentery and blood poisoning en route to the Dardanelles. In his last months he wrote The Soldier *and* The Dead, *representative of his generation of patriotic youth doomed to the trenches and gas warfare that were to come.*

Elizabeth Barrett Browning

'Yes,' I answered you last night:
'No,' this morning, sir, I say.
Colours seen by candle-night
Will not look the same by day.

The Lady's Yes

How I do love thee? Let me count the ways.

Sonnets from the Portuguese, 1850

Unless you can muse in a crowd all day
On the absent face that fixed you;
Unless you can love, as the angels may,
With the breadth of Heaven betwixt you:
Unless you can dream that his faith is fast,
Through behoving and unbehoving;
Unless you can die when the dream is past -
Oh, never call it loving:-

A Woman's Shortcomings

B *Elizabeth Barrett Browning (1806–61) the poet and wife of Robert, was the daughter of wealthy Edward Moulton Barrett. In youth she lived chiefly in Herefordshire, but eventually the family moved to Wimpole Street, London. Elizabeth began to write poetry and when a riding accident barred her for some years from an active life she gave her whole time to reading and writing. In 1844 she published* Verses, *a volume including* The Cry of the Children, *which made her name known. Because of her poetry Robert Browning visited her and fell in love with her. He married her in 1846, freeing her from a possessive father and sickroom existence.*

Robert Browning

The year's at the spring,
And day's at the morn;
Morning's at seven;
The hill-side's dew-pearled;
The lark's on the wing;
The snail's on the thorn;
God's in his heaven –
All's right with the world!

Pippa Passes: Morning

That's the wise thrush; he sings each song twice over,
Lest you should think he never could recapture
The first fine careless rapture!

Home-thoughts, from Abroad

Oh, to be in England
Now that April's there. . .

Home-thoughts, from Abroad

There may be Heaven; there must be hell;
Meantime, there is our earth here – well!

Time's Revenge

It was roses, roses, all the way.

The Patriot

Rats!
They fought the dogs and killed the cats,
And bit the babies in the cradles,
And ate the cheeses out of the vats,
And licked the soup from the cooks' own ladles.

The Pied Piper of Hamelin

And the mutterings grew to a grumbling,
And the grumbling grew to a mighty rumbling;
And out of the houses the rats came tumbling. . .

The Pied Piper of Hamelin

From street to street he piped, advancing,
And step by step they followed, dancing.

The Pied Piper of Hamelin

Robert Browning (1812–89), born in Camberwell, London, was the son of a clerk in the Bank of England. Educated at a private school and at home, he travelled a great deal in Europe. Devoting his whole life to poetry, he published his first piece Pauline *in 1833, but in 1835 his* Paracelsus *attracted the friendly notice of Carlyle, Wordsworth and other men of letters. He married Elizabeth Barrett and lived with her in Italy, but when she died he returned to London and published many more pieces of poetry.*

George Burns

My secret for longevity? Drinking martinis, smoking cigars.

Actually, it only takes one drink to get me loaded. Trouble is, I can't remember if it's the thirteenth or the fourteenth.

B Too bad that all the people who know how to run the country are busy driving taxicabs and cutting hair.

People ask what I'd most appreciate getting. I'll tell you: a paternity suit.

On his 87th birthday

George Burns (1898–), US comedian, began as a singer, then turned to vaudeville as a comic. Success came when he teamed up with Gracie Allen, touring America and Europe in the 20s, moving on to radio in the 30s and television in the 50s. He retired when Gracie, his wife, died in 1964 but began a new career as a film actor, when in 1976 at nearly eighty, he won an Academy Award for his performance as an ex-vaudeville performer in The Sunshine Boys.

Robert Burns

Should auld acquaintance be forgot,
And never brought to min'?

Auld Lang Syne

My love's like a red red rose
That's newly sprung in June.
My love's like the melodie
That's sweetly play'd in tune.

My Love is like a Red Red Rose

The best laid schemes o' mice an' men
Gang aft a-gley.

To a Mouse

Wee, sleekit, cow'rin', tim'rous beastie,
O, what a panic's in thy breastie!

To a Mouse

Robert Burns (1759–96) was the son of a Scottish small farmer. **B**
From 1784 to 1788 he farmed himself, but during that period he
wrote some of his best work - The Cotter's Saturday Night, The
Twa Dogs, Halloween, The Jolly Beggars, To a Mouse *and* To a
Mountain Daisy. *In 1786 he published the Kilmarnock edition of his*
early poems, which made him famous. A second edition of his poems
brought him £500, which enabled him to settle down on a small farm
and marry one of his many loves, Jean Armour. About the same time
he received an exciseman's appointment, and this became his principal
means of support. He died not knowing how popular Auld Lang Syne
would become.

Samuel Butler

Brigands demand your money or your life; women require both.

'Tis better to have loved and lost, than never to have lost at all.
The Way of All Flesh

Youth is like spring, an overpraised season.
The Way of All Flesh

There's many a good tune played on an old fiddle.
The Way of All Flesh

Samuel Butler (1835–1902), the philosophical English writer, emi-
grated as a sheep farmer to New Zealand after rowing with his
clergyman father over his attempts to become a painter. He returned
to Britain in 1864 and later wrote his satire Erehwon, *an inversion*
of Nowhere. His autobiography, The Way of All Flesh, *was pub-*
lished after his death. Acknowledging his wide-ranging attacks on the
beliefs of his day, he described himself as the enfant terrible *of litera-*
ture and science.

George Gordon Byron

Seek roses in December – ice in June;
Hope constancy in wind, or corn in chaff;

27

B Believe a woman or an epitaph,
Or any other thing that's false, before
You trust in critics, who themselves are sore.

English Bards and Scotch Reviewers

Maidens, like moths, are ever caught by glare.

Childe Harold's Pilgrimage

I stood in Venice, on the Bridge of Sighs,
A palace and a prison on each hand.

Childe Harold's Pilgrimage

There is a tide in the affairs of women
Which, taken at the flood, leads — God knows where.

Don Juan

What men call gallantry, and gods adultery,
Is much more common where the climate's sultry.

Don Juan

For the Angel of Death spreads his wings on the blast,
And breathed in the face of the foe as he pass'd.

Destruction of Sennacherib

George Gordon Noel Byron (1788–1824), sixth baron, was born in London with a club foot and brought up in poverty in Aberdeen by his mother, whose husband Captain John Byron had deserted her. Young Byron's fortunes changed when, at ten, he inherited the title of baron from his great uncle. He then went to Harrow and Trinity College, Cambridge. While at Cambridge he printed his Hours of Idleness. *A romantic figure, who was taken up and then dropped by London society, he had a series of disastrous love affairs. For several years he travelled abroad. He died of marsh fever fighting for Greek independence.*

Thomas Carlyle

The block of granite which was an obstacle in the pathway of the weak, became a stepping-stone in the pathway of the strong.

The three great elements of modern civilization, Gunpowder, Printing, and the Protestant Religion.

Critical and Miscellaneous Essays

Captains of industry.

Past and Present

Man is a tool-using animal. . .Without tools he is nothing, with tools he is all.

Sartor Resartus

No great man lives in vain. The history of the world is but the biography of great men.

Heroes and Hero Worship

Thomas Carlyle (1795–1881), Scottish historian and essayist, studied for the Presbyterian ministry but later gave up the Church and combined study of the law with miscellaneous literary work. He established his reputation as a literary genius with The French Revolution, *said to be still unrivalled in its vividness of narration.*

Hoagy Carmichael

The trouble with doing nothing is that you can never take any time off.

Hoagy Carmichael (1899–1982) was an American song composer and lyricist, best known for his Stardust *and* In the Cool, Cool, Cool of the Evening. *He was also a slow-speaking actor of light supporting roles, usually involving his singing at the piano. He wrote two autobiographies,* The Stardust Road *and* Sometimes I Wonder.

Lewis Carroll

'You are old, Father William,' the young man said,
'And your hair has become very white;
And yet you incessantly stand on your head –

C Do you think, at your age, it is right?'

'In my youth,' Father William replied to his son,
'I feared it might injure the brain;
But now that I'm perfectly sure I have none,
Why, I do it again and again.'

Alice's Adventures in Wonderland

The Queen was in a furious passion, and went stamping about, and shouting 'Off with his head!' or 'Off with her head!' about once in a minute.

Alice's Adventures in Wonderland

'Curiouser and curiouser!' cried Alice.

Alice's Adventures in Wonderland

'The time has come,' the Walrus said,
'To talk of many things:
Of shoes — and ships — and sealing wax
Of cabbages — and kings
And why the sea is boiling hot
And whether pigs have wings.'

Through the Looking-Glass

The rule is, jam to-morrow and jam yesterday – but never jam to-day.

Through the Looking-Glass

You see, it's like a portmanteau – there are two meanings packed up into one word.

Through the Looking-Glass

'Twas brillig and the slithy toves
Did gyre and gimble in the wabe.
All mincing were the borogoves
And the mome raths outgrabe.

Through the Looking-Glass: Jabberwocky

He would answer to 'Hi!' or to any loud cry,
Such as 'Fry me!' or 'Fritter my wig!'
To 'What-you-may-call-um!' or 'What-was-his-name!'
But especially 'Thing-um-a-jig!'

The Hunting of the Snark

Lewis Carroll (1832–98) was the pseudonym of Charles Lutwidge Dodgson, a mathematician and writer of children's books. He became a lecturer in mathematics at Oxford and published books on the subject, but became famous for Alice's Adventures in Wonderland. *This grew out of a story told by Dodgson to amuse three little girls, including the original Alice – Alice Liddell, daughter of the dean of Christ Church. Later he published* Through the Looking Glass *and* The Hunting of the Snark.

Jimmy Carter

I am convinced that UFOs exist, because I have seen one.

16.6.1976

I'm tired of taxing the poor people in our rich country and sending the money to rich people in poor countries.

On taxes, 29.8.1976

Jimmy Carter (James Earl Carter Jnr 1924–), American farmer and politician, was educated in Georgia and US Naval Academy, Annapolis. He served in the US Navy from 1946 to 1953 and attained the rank of Lieut-Commander. Then he built up the family peanut farming business, was State Senator of Georgia from 1962 to 1966; Governor of Georgia from 1971 to 1974; and President of the United States of America in January 1977. He stood for re-election in 1980 and was badly beaten by Ronald Reagan. He had been criticised for lacking in vision and his handling of the hostage taking of US embassy staff in Iran, which was a blow to national pride.

Barbara Cartland

When the (romantic) boom came and pornography began to fade

31

C in Sweden and Denmark and all the other countries, the one person who had '150 virgins' lying about was me.

I Search for Rainbows

There's no substitute for moonlight and kissing.

11.9.1977

Barbara Cartland (1901–), best-selling author of romantic fiction, had a governess before going to school and was a debutante. She turned her hand to writing after her father's death in Flanders in 1918 left the family short of money. She published her first novel at the age of twenty-one, which ran into five editions. Since then she has written hundreds of romantic novels as well as biographies, cookery books, plays, and some verse, and has organised charity events. She has also made frequent radio and television appearances.

Enrico Caruso

The requisite of a singer – a big chest, a big mouth, ninety per cent memory, ten per cent intelligence, lots of hard work, and something in the heart.

Enrico Caruso (1873–1921), was the eighteenth of twenty-one children of a poor Neopolitan family and the first to survive past infancy. He began singing in streets and churches. He made his first appearance on the Naples stage at twenty-one and later achieved great success in Milan as Puccini's La Bohème. *He won world-wide fame and appeared in many European and American cities, singing more than fifty operatic roles. He was one of the first singers to make gramophone records.*

Edith Cavell

I realise that patriotism is not enough. I must have no hatred or bitterness towards anyone.

Last words, 12.10.1915

Edith Louisa Cavell (1865–1915) was born in Norfolk. She was trained at the London Hospital and became matron of a medical institute in Brussels. During the German occupation she harboured wounded and refugee soldiers and aided their escape into Holland. Denounced by a renegade, she was tried by court martial and shot.

Miguel de Cervantes

Don't put too fine a point to your wit for fear it should get blunted.

The best sauce in the world is hunger.

Don Quixote

There are but two families in the world, as my grandmother used to say, the Haves and the Havenots.

Don Quixote

Blessings on him who invented sleep, the mantle that covers all human thoughts.

Don Quixote

Miguel de Cervantes (1547–1616) was a Spanish novelist and dramatist. Born at Alcala, the son of an apothecary, he lived for a time in Madrid and then went to Italy. In 1570 he became a soldier, but was taken prisoner by the Barbary pirates and spent five years as a prisoner at Algiers. Cervantes wrote a great deal of verse, a number of dramas, and the Exemplary Novels *which gave a good idea of the life of the time, but he is known best of all by his immortal novel* Don Quixote *which was published in two parts.*

Nicholas Chamfort

A day is wasted without laughter.

C Society is composed of two large classes; those who have more dinners than appetites, and those who have more appetite than dinners.

In great matters men try to show themselves to their best advantage; in small matters they show themselves as they are.

Sebastien Roch Nicholas Chamfort (1741–94) was a French writer and wit. At the outbreak of the Revolution he joined the Jacobins, took part in the storming of the Bastille, and bitterly attacked the National Convention. He mortally wounded himself when about to be arrested. He is best known for his Maximes, *which was published posthumously, but he was also author of comedies, literary criticisms, letters and verse.*

G.K. Chesterton

The home is not the one tame place in the world of adventure. It is the one wild place in the world of rules and set tasks.

There are no rules of architecture for a castle in the clouds.

A yawn is a silent shout.

Democracy means government by the uneducated, while aristocracy means government by the badly educated.
New York Times, 1931

There is something wrong with a man if he does not want to break the Ten Commandments.
Quoted in Observer, 1925

The rich are the scum of the earth in every country.
The Flying Inn

Gilbert Keith Chesterton (1874–1936) was a British author, born in **C**
London. He studied art, but quickly turned to journalism. In poetry
his best work was in satire, particularly in his Wine, Water and Song
and The Ballad of the White Horse. *His most famous novels are those*
dealing with the adventures of the naive priest-detective, Father Brown.

Sir Winston Churchill

I felt as if I were walking with destiny and that all my past life
had been but a preparation for this hour and this trial.

The Gathering Storm

I cannot forecast to you the action of Russia. It is a riddle wrapped
in a mystery inside an enigma.

Broadcast, 1.10.1939

I have nothing to offer but blood, toil, tears and sweat. ✓

Speech in House of Commons, 13.5.1940

We shall not flag or fail. We shall fight in France, we shall fight
on the seas and the oceans, we shall fight with growing confidence
and growing strength in the air, we shall defend our island, whatever the cost may be. . .

Speech in House of Commons, 4.6.1940

Let us therefore brace ourselves to our duty and so bear ourselves
that if the British Empire and its Commonwealth last for a thousand years men will still say, 'This was their finest hour.'

Speech in the House of Commons, 18.6.1940

The gratitude of every home in our island, in our Empire, and
indeed throughout the world, except in the abodes of the guilty,
goes out to the British airmen who, undaunted by odds, unwearied
in their constant challenge and mortal danger, are turning the tide

C of the world war by their prowess and by their devotion. Never in the field of human conflict was so much owed by so many to so few.

Speech in the House of Commons, 20.8.1940

These two great organisations of the English-speaking democracies, the British Empire and the United States, will have to be somewhat mixed up together in some of their affairs . . . I do not view the process with any misgivings. I could not stop it if I wished; no one can stop it. Like the Mississippi, it just keeps rolling along. Let it roll. Let it roll on full flood, inexorable, irresistible, benignant, to broader lands and better days.

Speech in House of Commons, 20.8.1940

Give us the tools, and we will finish the job.

Broadcast address, 9.2.1941

It becomes still more difficult to reconcile Japanese action with prudence or even with sanity. What kind of people do they think we are?

Speech to US Congress after Pearl Harbor, 26.12.1941

When I warned them [the French Government] that Britain would fight on alone whatever they did their generals told their Prime Minister and his divided Cabinet, 'In three weeks England will have had her neck wrung like a chicken.' Some chicken! some neck!

Speech to Canadian Parliament, 30.12.1941

An iron curtain has descended across the Continent.

Speech at Fulton, USA, 5.3.1946

To jaw-jaw is better than to war-war.

Speech in Washington, 26.6.1954

Sir Winston Leonard Spencer Churchill (1874–1965) was a descendant of the great Duke of Marlborough. Churchill was born at Blenheim Palace, the elder son of Lord Randolph Churchill and his American wife, Jenny Jerome. During the Boer War he was the war correspondent of the Morning Post, *was taken prisoner, then made a dramatic escape from imprisonment to Pretoria.*

In 1900 Churchill was elected Conservative MP for Oldham – but he disagreed with Chamberlain's tariff reform policy and joined the

*Liberals. Later he became President of the Board of Trade, and intro-
duced legislation for the establishment of Labour Exchanges. In 1910
he became Home Secretary and was present at the siege of Sidney Street.*

*As First Lord of the Admiralty he became involved in controversy over
the Dardanelles operation, and in 1916 was in the trenches of France
with the Royal Scots Fusiliers. As Minister of Munitions under Lloyd
George, he had much to do with the development of the tank.*

*In the 1930s he was the voice in the political wilderness warn-
ing against the growing Nazi menace. When Chamberlain resigned
in 1940, Churchill formed the wartime coalition and convinced the
country the war could be won. He forged the alliance with Roosevelt's
United States and Stalin's Russia that defeated the Axis. Although
defeated electorally at the end of the war, he led the Conservative
government of 1951–55, when he retired at eighty. He was knighted
in 1952. Churchill was also a distinguished writer. He won the Nobel
Prize for Literature in 1953.*

Arthur Hugh Clough

Do not adultery commit;
Advantage rarely comes of it.

The Latest Decalogue

Grace is given of God, but knowledge is bought in the market.

The Bothie of Tober-na-Vuolich

When daylight comes, comes in the light,
In front the sun climbs slow, how slowly,
But westward, look, the land is bright.

Say not the Struggle Naught Availeth

*Arthur Hugh Clough (1819–61), the British poet, was born in Liv-
erpool, the son of a rich cotton merchant, and was at Rugby under
the famous Doctor Arnold. His poem* Say not the Struggle Naught
Availeth *was made famous during World War II because it was quoted
by Sir Winston Churchill in one of his war speeches.*

S.T. Coleridge

In Xanadu did Kubla Khan
A stately pleasure-dome decree:
Where Alph, the sacred river, ran

C Through caverns measureless to man
Down to a sunless sea.

Kubla Khan

As idle as a painted ship
Upon a painted ocean.

The Rime of the Ancient Mariner

Water, water, everywhere,
And all the boards did shrink;
Water, water, everywhere,
Nor any drop to drink.

The Rime of the Ancient Mariner

They stood aloft, the scars remaining,
Like cliffs which had been rent asunder. . .

Christabel

The Knight's bones are dust,
And his good sword rust -
His soul is with the saints, I trust.

The Knight's Tomb

Samuel Taylor Coleridge (1772–1834), the English poet and supreme critic of the Romantic movement, was the son of the vicar of Ottery St Mary, Devon. He was educated at Christ's Hospital and Jesus College, Cambridge. He contributed verses to the Morning Chronicle *and collaborated with Wordsworth in* Lyrical Ballads, *which contained his* Ancient Mariner. *In 1798 he visited Germany, where he became interested in German literature and philosophy. The best of his criticism is found in* Biographia Literaria *and* Table Talk. *His poetry drew on mythology, dream images and drug-induced fantasy.*

Confucius

If husband sent too often to doghouse, he go at last to cathouse.

Man has three ways of acting wisely: Firstly, on meditation, this is the noblest; Secondly, on imitation, this is the easiest; and thirdly, on experience: This is the bitterest.

What you do not want done to yourself, do not do to others. **C**

To be wronged is nothing unless you continue to remember it.

Everything has its beauty, but not everyone sees it.

Confucius (c550–478BC) is a Latinised form of K'ung Fu-tzu (K'ung the master) and this Chinese sage was born in Lu, a small state in what later became the province of Shangtun. His early years were spent in poverty, but at fifteen his mind was set on learning. Gradually he attracted a number of disciples to his system of cosmology, politics and ethics. He revised the ancient Chinese scriptures, and on his death was buried with great pomp.

William Congreve

Music hath charms to soothe a savage breast,
To soften rocks, or bend a knotted oak.
The Mourning Bride

Heav'n has no rage, like love to hatred turn'd,
Nor Hell a fury like a woman scorn'd.
The Mourning Bride

Defer not till to-morrow to be wise.
To-morrow's sun to thee may never rise.
Letter to Viscount Cobham

William Congreve (1670–1729) was born near Leeds, was a friend of Swift at Trinity College, Dublin, and then studied law in London. He won immediate success with his first comedy The Old Bachelor *and this was followed by* The Double Dealer, Love for Love *and his tragedy* The Mourning Bride. *His masterpiece* The Way of the World *was at first regarded as a failure. Congreve is regarded by many people as the most brilliant of the Restoration comic dramatists.*

Cyril Connolly

Whom the Gods wish to destroy they first call promising.

The man who is master of his passions is reason's slave.

39

C Imprisoned in every fat man a thin one is wildly signalling to be let out.

Cyril Connolly (1903–74), British journalist, was born in Coventry and went to Eton and Oxford on scholarships. He wrote regularly for The Sunday Times *and various periodicals like the* New Statesman. *In 1939 he co-founded the literary magazine* Horizon *and edited it until 1950. He also wrote a dozen books and was interested in short novels.*

Joseph Conrad

You shall judge of a man by his foes as well as by his friends.

Lord Jim

The mind of man is capable of anything — because everything is in it, all the past as well as all the future.

Heart of Darkness

Joseph Conrad (Teodor Josef Konrad Korzeniowski (1857–1924) was born of Polish parents in the Ukraine, and accompanied them when they were exiled to northern Russia. For a time he went to school in Cracow, but in 1874 he became a member of the crew of a French vessel, which satisfied a long-felt craving for a seafaring life. In 1884 he was naturalised as a British subject. In 1894 he left the sea and devoted himself to literature. His Lord Jim *was an overlooked masterpiece rediscovered by readers after another book,* Chance, *had brought him success.*

Shirley Conran

If you don't shake the tree a bit, the golden apples of good luck might not fall into your lap.

Futurewoman, 1981

Life is too short to stuff a mushroom.

Superwoman, 1975

*Shirley Conran (1932–), journalist and author, is the eldest of six chil-
dren. She trained as a sculptor and studied painting. Having worked
as a designer for ten years, she became home editor of the* Daily Mail
and then its women's editor. She wrote Superwoman *in 1974 and was
immediately hailed as a modern Mrs Beeton. In 1982 she ventured into
fiction with* Lace, *a further bestseller.*

Sir Noel Coward

The Stately Homes of England
How Beautiful they stand,
To prove the upper classes
Have still the upper hand.

The Stately Homes of England

Mad dogs and Englishmen go out in the midday sun.

Mad Dogs and Englishmen

Don't put your daughter on the stage, Missis Worthington
Don't put your daughter on the stage.

Mrs Worthington

We have no reliable guarantee that the afterlife will be any less
exasperating than this one, have we?

Blithe Spirit

*Sir Noel Coward (1899–1973), English dramatist, actor and com-
poser, was born at Teddington into a musical family. He first
appeared on stage at eleven, an early start to his career in theatre,
films, revues and short stories. His sophisticated wit endeared him to
audiences on both sides of the Atlantic for often revived comedies like*
Private Lives *and* Blithe Spirit. *After the war and his patriotic film*
In Which We Serve, *he specialised in cabaret. He was knighted in
1970.*

William Cowper

Now stir the fire, and close the shutters fast,
Let fall the curtains, wheel the sofa round.

The Task – Winter Evening

C To-morrow is our wedding-day,
And then we shall repair
Unto the Bell at Edmonton
All in a chaise and pair.

John Gilpin

O'erjoy'd was he to find
That, though on pleasure she was bent,
She had a frugal mind.

John Gilpin

How much a dunce that has been sent to roam
Excels a dunce that has been kept at home.

The Progress of Error

A fool must now and then be right by chance.

Conversation

God moves in a mysterious way.

Olney Hymns

Twelve years have elapsed since I last took a view
Of my favourite field, and the bank where they [poplars] grew;
And now in the grass behold they are laid,
And the tree is my seat that once lent me a shade.

The Poplar-Field

William Cowper (1731–1800), the English poet who wrote of the joys of eighteenth-century country life, first studied law. He turned to religion when recovering from a bout of mental illness and began his literary work with the hymns he wrote with the Reverend John Newton. Later Mrs Unwin persuaded him to write poetry, and a volume of poems appeared in 1782. Lady Austen told him the story of John Gilpin, which became the subject of one of his most popular poems, and she also persuaded him to write his greatest work The Task.

Quentin Crisp

The lie is the basic building block of good manners.

Manners From Heaven

42

As soon as I stepped out of my mother's womb on to dry land, I Crealized that I had made a mistake — that I shouldn't have come, but the trouble with children is that they are not returnable.

The Naked Civil Servant

I don't hold with abroad and think that foreigners speak English when our backs are turned.

The Naked Civil Servant

An autobiography is an obituary in serial form with the last instalment missing.

The Naked Civil Servant

My father won his great gamble with the future. He died.

The Naked Civil Servant

Quentin Crisp (1908–) was born Denis Pratt in Surrey and changed his name in 1977 when he emigrated from England to New York. A writer who first worked as an artist's model and then as a stage actor, he is best known for his autobiographical The Naked Civil Servant *published in 1968, which relates his social and psychological hardships as a homosexual as well as his witty perceptions of life. He also wrote two novels and continued his wit in non-fictional form.*

Oliver Cromwell

What shall we do with this bauble? There, take it away.

Of the Mace, when dismissing Parliament, 20.4.1653

Mr. Lely, I desire you would use all your skill to paint my picture truly like me, and not flatter me at all; but remark all these roughnesses, pimples, warts, and everything as you see me, otherwise I will never pay a farthing for it.

Remark: Walpole's Anecdotes of Painting

C *Oliver Cromwell (1599–1658) Puritan leader of the parliamentary army in the English civil war, was born in Huntingdon, the son of a small landowner, and educated at the local grammar school and Cambridge. Active in the events leading to the Civil War, he raised a troop of horse and was engaged in the Battle of Edgehill. After that he raised more cavalry forces, which were chiefly responsible for the victory at Marston Moor. Cromwell was a member of the special commission which tried the King and condemned him to death, and later he assumed the title of Protector, with almost royal powers.*

W.H. Davies

What is this life if, full of care,
We have no time to stand and stare?
No time to stand beneath the boughs
And stare as long as sheep or cows.

Leisure

Welcome to you, rich Autumn days,
Here comes the cold, leaf-picking wind,
When golden stocks are seen in fields –
All standing arm-in-arm entwined.

Rich Days

I love thee for a heart that's kind –
Not for the knowledge in thy mind.

William Henry Davies (1871–1940), the British poet, went to America and for years lived the life of a hobo. He lost his right foot while 'riding the rods', and later returned to England and published his first volume of poems Soul's Destroyer. *While living the life of a wandering pedlar he published more volumes of simple verse and the prose work* The Autobiography of a Supertramp.

Bette Davis

Morality to me is honesty, integrity, character. Old-fashioned words. There are new words now that excuse everything.

She's the original good time that was had by all.

Of a starlet

Give me the days of heroes and villains. The people you can bravo or hiss. There was a truth to them that all the slick credulity of today cannot touch.

D *Bette Davis (1908–), the American actress and film star, was born Ruth Elizabeth Davis in Massachusetts. She entered films in 1930 and established her reputation with* Of Human Bondage. *Later films included* Dangerous *and* Jezebel, *both of which earned her Academy Awards. Her career has been an outstanding one and she has written two autobiographies,* The Lonely Life *(1962) and* Mother Goddam *(1975). She has specialised in melodrama, often portraying intensely emotional women.*

Sammy Davis Junior

I invented controversy, but not on purpose.

My own rules are very simple. Don't hurt nobody. Be nice to people.

I'm a coloured, one–eyed Jew — do I need anything else?

Yes I Can

Sammy Davis Junior (1925–) was born into an American vaudeville family and began singing and dancing in his father's act at four. From the family night club act, he graduated to a solo career in Broadway musicals and Hollywood films in the 1950s and 60s. He wrote the autobiographical Yes I Can *and* Hollywood in a Suitcase *in 1980.*

Daniel Defoe

The good die early, and the bad die late.

Character of the Late Dr S. Annesley

He bade me observe it, and I should always find, that the calamities of life were shared among the upper and the lower part of mankind; but that the middle station had the fewest disasters.

Robinson Crusoe

Wherever God erects a house of prayer,
The Devil always builds a chapel there;
And 'twill be found upon examination,
The latter has the largest congregation.

The True-born Englishman

46

Daniel Defoe (1660–1731) was born in London, the son of James Foe, **D**
a butcher, but later he changed his name by adding the prefix. Daniel
took part in Monmouth's rebellion, then joined William III's army in
1688. His early writings were political pamphlets and satirical poems,
including in 1702 a notorious pamphlet entitled The Shortest Way
with the Dissenters. *For this he was fined, imprisoned and pilloried.*
This harsh treatment affected his behaviour, making him mistrustful
and mercenary. Only at fifty-nine did he start his novels, producing the
immortal Robinson Crusoe *as well as* Moll Flanders *and* A Journal
of the Plague Year.

Charles De Gaulle

The French will only be united under the threat of danger. No
one can bring together in cold blood a country which has 265 types
of cheese.

1951

Since a politician never believes what he says, he is surprised
when others believe him.

Newsweek, 1962

When I want to know what France thinks, I ask myself.

Sons of France, 1966

General Charles De Gaulle (1890–1970), French military and pol-
itical leader, graduated from the national military academy of St Cyr
and fought in World War I. His criticism of France's reliance on fixed
fortifications was proved right when Germany outflanked the Maginot
Line in 1940. He escaped to London, becoming Free French Resistance
leader. He briefly ruled liberated France, then retired until called back
in 1958 as the only man who could save France from civil war. He
survived several assassination attempts in eleven years as President.

Walter De La Mare

Very old are we men;
Our dreams are tales

D Told in dim Eden
By Eve's nightingales.

All That's Past

Oh, no man knows
Through what wild centuries
Roves back the rose.

All That's Past

Walter De La Mare (1873–1956), English poet and novelist, was born in Kent. After eighteen years as an office worker, he turned to writing and produced a prodigious number of stories, ranging from the occult to romance. He delighted children and grown-ups alike with his whimsical rhymes and verse.

Lord Denning

The law is not an ass, at all events when I try and enunciate it.

People sometimes think we're asleep when they see us in the House of Lords, but what really happens is we're leaning back because there's a loudspeaker at the end of each seat.

TV interview, 1982

Alfred Thompson Denning (1899–), created a life peer in 1957, was England's longest serving judge. He was called to the bar in 1923 with an outstanding university record. For thirty of his thirty-eight years as judge, he was Master of the Rolls. In 1963 he headed the enquiry into the Profumo scandal. At eighty-nine, still outspoken, he took to the other side of the bench, advocating in a legal case to keep local footpaths open.

Charles Dickens

Annual income twenty pounds, annual expenditure nineteen nineteen six, result happiness. Annual income twenty pounds, annual expenditure twenty pounds ought and six, result misery.

David Copperfield, Mr Micawber

Polly put the kettle on, we'll all have tea.

Barnaby Rudge

'God bless us every one!' cried Tiny Tim, the last of all.

'When a man says he's willin',' said Mr Barkis. . . 'it is as much as to say, that a man's waitin' for a answer.'

David Copperfield

Oliver Twist has asked for more!

Bumble in Oliver Twist

Train up a fig-tree in the way it should go, and when you are old sit under the shade of it.

Dombey and Son, Captain Cuttle

O let us love our occupations,
Bless the squire and his relations,
Live upon our daily rations,
And always know our proper stations.

A Christmas Book for Children, The Chimes

Youth are boarded, clothed, booked, furnished with pocket-money, provided with all necessaries, instructed in all languages living and dead, mathematics, orthography, geometry, astronomy, trigonometry, the use of the globes, algebra, single stick (if required), writing, arithmetic, fortification, and every other branch of classical literature. Terms, twenty guineas per annum. No extras, no vacations, and diet unparalleled.

Nicholas Nickleby, Mr Squeers's Academy

With affection beaming in one eye, and calculation shining out of the other.

Martin Chuzzlewit, Mrs Todgers

Miss Bolo rose from the table considerably agitated, and went straight home, in a flood of tears and a sedan chair.

Pickwick Papers

It's over, and can't be helped, and that's one consolation as they always say in Turkey, ven they cuts the wrong man's head off.

Pickwick Papers, Sam Weller

Accidents will occur in the best-regulated families.

David Copperfield, Mr Micawber

D It is a far, far better thing that I do, than I have ever done; it is a far, far better rest I go to, than I have ever known.
A Tale of Two Cities, Sidney Carton

I think . . . that it is the best club in London.
Our Mutual Friend, Mr Twemlow on the House of Commons

Charles Dickens (1812–70), considered the greatest English novelist of the Victorian period, drew on the injustices and insecurities of his own unhappy childhood. His middle–class father, a government clerk, was imprisoned for debt and Charles, the eldest son, had to leave school to work in a squalid factory. Finally gaining further schooling, he became a lawyer's clerk, then a reporter in Doctors' Commons, and eventually parliamentary reporter for the Morning Chronicle, *to which he contributed his* Sketches by Boz. *His* Pickwick Papers *were originally intended as an accompaniment to a series of sporting illustrations, but the adventures of Pickwick outgrew their setting and established Dickens' position as a writer.*

Marlene Dietrich

The average man is more interested in a woman who is interested in him than he is in a woman – any woman – with beautiful legs.

Most women set out to try to change a man, and when they have changed him they do not like him.

Marlene Dietrich (1901–) was born in Berlin as Maria Magdalena von Losch. A German singer-actress living in America for many years, she became a legend of glamour in films, being known particularly for her part in The Blue Angel.

Benjamin Disraeli

Though I sit down now, the time will come when you will hear me.
Maiden Speech, 7.12.1837

The right hon. Gentleman [Sir Robert Peel] caught the Whigs bathing, and walked away with their clothes.
Speech in House of Commons, 28.2.1845

The question is this: is man an ape or an angel? Now I am on the side of the angels.

Speech, Oxford 25.11.1864

No, it is better not. She would only ask me to take a message to Albert.

Reply when it was suggested to him as he lay dying that he might like a visit from Queen Victoria

Every woman should marry – and no man.

Lothair

Benjamin Disraeli (1804–81), first Earl of Beaconsfield, was one of the great Victorian statesmen, and bought for Britain a controlling interest in the Suez Canal. He was the eldest son of Isaac D'Israeli and received his literary training chiefly in his father's library instead of at university. He published his first novel Vivian Grey *in his twenty-second year. Though hampered by debt, he made the popular grand tour, and published* The Young Duke *in 1831. In 1837 he entered Parliament as Member for Maidstone, and in a few years became the leader of a small group called The Young England Party, whose ideas are described in his novels* Coningsby *and* Tancredi. *In his last year as prime minister, 1880, he published his last novel* Endymion.

Dorothy Dix

Drying a widow's tears is one of the most dangerous occupations known to man.

Dorothy Dix (Dorothy Knight Waddy, 1909–70) was the second daughter of William Knight Dix. Educated at St Christopher's School, Hampstead, Lausanne University and University College, London, she became a QC in 1957 and a County Court Judge in 1968. She acted as Deputy-Recorder of Deal in 1946, during the absence of Mr Christmas Humphries at the Tokyo War trials.

Henry Austin Dobson

The ladies of St. James's!
They're painted to the eyes,

D Their white it stays for ever,
Their red it never dies.

The Ladies of St. James's

Time goes, you say? Ah no!
Alas, time stays, we go.

The Paradox of Time

Henry Austin Dobson (1840–1921) was an accomplished writer of light verse, and some of his best work appeared in Vignettes in Rhyme, Proverbs in Porcelain *and* Old World Idylls.

John Donne

No man is an Island, entire of itself; every man is a piece of the Continent, a part of the main; if a clod be washed away by the sea, Europe is the lesser, as well as if a promontory were, as well as if a manor of thy friends or thine own were: any man's death diminishes me, because I am involved in Mankind; and therefore never send to know for whom the bell tolls: it tolls for thee.

Meditation

Come live with me, and be my love
And we will some new pleasures prove
Of golden sands, and crystal brooks,
With silken lines, and silver hooks.

The Bait

John Donne (1572–1631), English metaphysical poet and preacher, was a tradesman's son. He began writing poetry about love affairs as a law student. After various adventures abroad on naval expeditions, he turned to more spiritual matters. He rejected his Catholic background and took holy orders in the Church of England.

Feodor Mikhailovitch Dostoievsky

Man is a pliable animal, a being who gets accustomed to everything.

The House of the Dead

Feodor Miklhailovitch Dostoievsky (1821–81) was born in Moscow
and educated as an engineer, but soon he began to write. His first book
Poor Folk *was published in 1846, but his political activities led to his*
arrest and he was sent to Siberia, where he remained for four years.
The next three were spent in the army, and after that he spent his time
in writing and travelling. His major novels are Crime and Punishment, The Idiot, The Devils *and* The Brothers Karamazov.

Sir Arthur Conan Doyle

It is an old maxim of mine that when you have excluded the
impossible, whatever remains, however improbable, must be the
truth.

The Beryl Coronet

You know my method. It is founded upon the observance of trifles.
The Boscombe Valley Mystery

You know my methods, Watson.

The Crooked Man

Sir Arthur Conan Doyle (1859–1930) wrote A Study in Scarlet *in*
1887, featuring a detective called Sherlock Holmes, to supplement his
earnings as a doctor. Although his historical novels were personally more
important to him, the deductive powers of Sherlock Holmes, aided by
the amiable Dr Watson, captured his still enormous readership. He
was knighted in 1902 for medical services during the Boer War. After
his son died from World War I wounds, he became a spiritualist.

John Dryden

All human things are subject to decay,
And, when fate summons, monarchs must obey.

Mac Flecknoe

None but the brave deserves the fair.

Alexander's Feast

Happy the man, and happy he alone,
He who can call today his own:

53

D He who, secure within, can say,
To-morrow do thy worst, for I have lived to-day.

Translation of Horace

John Dryden (1631–1700), exponent of heroic tragedy, was born at Aldwinkle, Northants, and went to London in 1657. In 1659 he published Heroic Stanzas *in memory of Oliver Cromwell, but he hastened to celebrate the Restoration with* Astraea Redux. *He produced many plays and much other work, but at the Revolution of 1688 was deprived of the laureateship to which he had been appointed in 1668 because he was a Roman Catholic. Dryden was the greatest English literary figure of his age.*

Marie Jeanne Becu Du Barry

After all, the world is but an amusing theatre, and I see no reason why a pretty woman should not play a principal part in it.

We learn to howl in the society of wolves.

Marie Jeanne Becu Du Barry (1743–93), daughter of a dressmaker, married the Comte Guillaume Du Barry and was presented at Court, where she soon became mistress of Louis XV of France. She is said to have been strikingly handsome, not without wit, and frank to the point of vulgarity. She exercised great influence on Louis, but on his death she was banished to a convent. At the Revolution she fled to London, but returned to Paris in 1793, when she was arrested and guillotined.

Thomas Alva Edison

Genius is one per cent inspiration and ninety-nine per cent perspiration.

Newspaper interview in Life, 1932

As a cure for worrying, work is better than whisky.

Show me a thoroughly satisfied man — and I will show you a failure.

Thomas Alva Edison (1847–1931), American electrician and inventor, was born at Milan, Ohio, of mixed Dutch and Scottish descent. In early life a telegraph operator, his inventive genius soon showed itself in the series of experiments into the improvement of electrical transmission. He played a large part in the development of incandescent lamps, electric light and trains, plus a central system for electrical generation and distribution. He took out more than 1,000 patents for his discoveries.

Albert Einstein

If A is success in life, then A equals X plus Y plus Z.
Work is X; Y is play; and Z is keeping your mouth shut.

I also am a revolutionary, though only a scientific one.

I cannot believe that God plays dice with the universe.

Nationalism is an infantile disease. It is the measles of mankind.

The World As I See It

E *Professor Albert Einstein (1879–1955), a German-Swiss physicist, framed the theories of relativity that transformed human understanding of time and space. After teaching at the Polytechnic School in Zurich he became a Swiss citizen and was appointed an inspector of patents at Berne. In his spare time he obtained his PhD at Zurich, and some of his papers on physics were of such a high standard that in 1909 he was given a chair of theoretical physics at the University. His first theory – the so-called special theory of relativity – was published in 1905. In 1915 he issued his general theory. He received the Nobel Prize for Physics in 1921 for his work in quantum theory. When Hitler came to power in Germany, he emigrated from Berlin to America, where he often spoke out against nuclear weapons.*

George Eliot

You love the roses – so do I. I wish
The sky would rain down roses, as they rain
From off the shaken bush. . .
. . . Why will it not?
Then all the valley would be pink and white
And soft to tread on.

The Book of a Thousand Poems, Roses

George Eliot (1819–80) was the pseudonym of the British writer Mary Ann Evans. Born at Chilvers Coton, Warwickshire, she received a strictly evangelical upbringing but later moved to Coventry and was converted to free thinking. She became famous for her novels Adam Bede, The Mill on the Floss *and* Silas Marner, *which were all set in her native county and analysed provincial society. Other novels followed;* Middlemarch *is regarded as her finest work and one of the greatest novels of the century.*

T.S. Eliot

The winter evening settles down
With smells of steaks in passageways.
Six o'clock.
The burnt-out ends of smoky days.

Preludes

This is the way the world ends,
Not with a bang but a whimper.

The Hollow Men

Thomas Stearns Eliot (1888–1965), American-born and educated at Harvard, moved to Britain at twenty-six and later became a British subject. He mixed with the Bloomsbury Set and, while working for a bank, wrote verse that led from The Waste Land *and* Four Quartets, Murder in the Cathedral *and* The Cocktail Party. *He won the Nobel Prize for Literature in 1948.*

Elizabeth I, Queen of England

If thy heart fails thee, climb not at all.
Lines written on a window after Sir Walter Raleigh's own 'Fain would I climb, yet fear to fall'

I know I have the body of a weak and feeble woman, but I have the heart and stomach of a king, and of a king of England too.
Speech to the Troops at Tilbury on the approach of the Armada, 1588

Elizabeth I (1533–1603), Queen of England and the daughter of Henry VIII and Anne Boleyn, was born at Greenwich. During Mary's reign Elizabeth's Protestant sympathies brought her under suspicion, and she lived at Hatfield until she became Queen in 1558. Her reign lasted forty-five years, and its glories are one of the main themes of English history.

David Everett

Don't view me with a critic's eye,
But pass my imperfections by.
Large streams from little fountains flow,
Tall oaks from little acorns grow.

Lines written for a School Declamation

David Everett (1770–1813) was an American author. Born at Princetown, Massachusetts, he became a lawyer and journalist, and was the author of Common Sense in Dishabille, Daranzel *(a play performed in 1798 and 1800) and several other works.*

F Gracie Fields

People are always sending me pictures of their aspidistras.

10.9.1978

Gracie Fields (1898–1979) was an English comedienne. Born Gracie Stansfield in Rochdale, she appeared in London in Mr. Tower of London, *which gave over 4,000 performances. Later she became a popular motion-picture actress and singer.*

W.C. Fields

Smile first thing in the morning. Get it over with.

I'm allergic to water. My grandmother drowned me in the filthy stuff.

In Edgar Bergen's 'Chase and Sanborn Radio Show'

I am free of all prejudice. I hate everyone equally.

Saturday Review, 1967

If at first you don't succeed, try, try again. Then quit. There's no use being a damn fool about it.

Never trust your wife behind your back, even if she claims she only wants to wash or scratch it.

Give a woman a hundred dollars in small bills and it won't last long. But a hundred dollar bill she'll hold on to for dear life. She'll keep postponing breaking it. Therefore you won't have to replenish her coffers for a long time.

On the occasion of Carlotta Monti's birthday

W.C. (Claude) Fields (1880–1946), sad-faced American comedian, was born in Philadelphia into a poor family named Dukinfield and ran away from home at the age of eleven. In July 1897 he obtained his first professional employment as a 'tramp juggler' in an open-air theatre near Norristown, Pennsylvania. He soon did well in vaudeville and later on screen.

F. Scott Fitzgerald

Let me tell you about the very rich. They are different from you and me.

The Rich Boy

There are only the pursued, the pursuing, the busy, and the tired. **F**
The Great Gatsby

In a real dark night of the soul it is always three o'clock in the morning, day after day.
The Crack Up

Show me a hero and I will write you a tragedy.
The Last Tycoon

Francis Scott Fitzgerald (1896–1940), American novelist and short story writer, had a chequered sojourn at Princeton University and joined the army. He fell in love with Zelda Sayre, daughter of an Alabama Supreme Court judge. The rise and fall of their marriage and expatriate life-style featured in his work. After her mental breakdown and his destructive drinking as a has-been, he was involved with Hollywood columnist Sheilah Graham. His best known novels were The Great Gatsby, Tender is the Night *and* The Last Tycoon.

James Elroy Flecker

I have seen old ships sail like swans asleep
Beyond the village which men still call Tyre.
The Old Ships

Away, for we are ready to a man!
Our camels sniff the evening and are glad.
Lead on, O Master of the Caravan:
Lead on the Merchant Princes of Bagdad.
The Golden Journey to Samarkand

Have we not Indian carpets dark as wine,
Turbans and sashes, gowns and bows and veils,
And broideries of intricate design,
And printed hangings in enormous bales?
The Golden Journey to Samarkand

Sweet to ride forth at evening from the wells,
When shadows pass gigantic on the sand,

F And softly through the silence beat the bells
Along the Golden Road to Samarkand.
The Golden Journey to Samarkand

James Elroy Flecker (1884–1915), English poet and novelist, entered the Consular service and was posted first to Constantinople and then to Beirut. He published The Bridge of Fire, Forty-Two Poems, The Golden Journey to Samarkand *and* The Old Ships. *Two plays,* Hassan *and* Don Juan, *were published posthumously.*

Michael Foot

I had better recall, before someone else does, that I said on one occasion that all was fair in love, war, and parliamentary procedure.
7.9.1975

What politics is all about is to try to combine protection of your principles with effective action. It is no use having effective action if you do not protect your principles.
On being voted Leader of the Labour Party, 10.11.1980

The Right Hon. Michael Foot (1913–), son of the late Sir Isaac Foot, has been MP for Ebbw Vale since 1960. He became Deputy Leader of the Labour Party in 1976 and was voted Leader of the Opposition upon the resignation of James Callaghan in 1980. He resigned when his party was badly defeated in the 1983 elections. He held the post of assistant editor of the Tribune *in 1937/8, was acting editor of the* Evening Standard *in 1942, and political columnist of the* Daily Herald *from 1944 until 1964.*

Henry Ford

√ History is bunk.
In the witness box during his libel suit vs the Chicago Tribune, July 1919

I did not say it was bunk. It was bunk to me.
Allan Nevins, 'Ford: Expansion and Challenge'

Exercise is bunk. If you are healthy, you don't need it. If you are sick, you shouldn't take it.

Money is like an arm or a leg — use it or lose it.

New York Times 1931

You can have any colour you like, as long as it is black.

When discussing the specification of his cars

Luck and destiny are the excuses of the world's failures.

6.3.1927

Henry Ford (1863–1947), American industrialist born at Greenfield, Michigan, developed an early interest in mechanics. He experimented in motor-car manufacture and started the business that grew into the Ford Motor Company in Detroit. Its assembly-line technique was able to turn out the first cheap, mass-produced car. More than fifteen million Model T Fords were sold between 1909 and 1927. In 1914 he instituted a scheme of profit-sharing. With his son, Edsel, he engaged in tractor manufacture, and in 1940 set up the Willow Run bomber aircraft plant which became vital to the Allied war effort.

St Francis of Assissi

Lord, make us instruments of thy peace. Where there is hatred, let us sow love; where there is injury, pardon; where there is discord, union; where there is doubt, faith; where there is despair, hope; where there is darkness, light; where there is sadness, joy.

St Francis (1162–1226) was born in Assissi, the son of a rich silk merchant. He spent his youth seeking pleasure. Visions of Christ changed his life in his early twenties. He devoted himself to the sick and lived in poverty, disinherited by his father as a madman. Many stories are told of his ability to charm wild animals and to influence men in all walks of life.

Benjamin Franklin

Three may keep a secret, if two of them are dead.

Remember that time is money.

We must indeed all hang together, or most assuredly, we shall all hang separately.

At US Declaration of Independence, 1776

F Here Skugg lies snug
As a bug in a rug.
On the death of a friend's squirrel

Thinks I, that man has an axe to grind.
Pennsylvania Almanac, 1758

There never was a good war or a bad peace.
Letter to Joseph Quincey, 1773

Benjamin Franklin (1706–90), American statesman and scientist, was the fifteenth of seventeen children of a Boston tallow chandler. Largely self-educated and apprenticed to a printer, he went on to journalism and became owner of the Pennsylvania Gazette. *After experimenting with electrical phenomena, he became interested in politics, trying to reconcile England with its American colonies. Unable to achieve this, he helped draw up the Declaration of Independence and later the US constitution.*

Robert Frost

Home is the place where, when you have to go there, they have to take you in.

A poem begins in delight and ends in wisdom.

All men are born free and equal – free at least in their right to be different. Some people want to homogenize society everywhere. I'm against the homogenizers in art, in politics, in every walk of life. I want the cream to rise.
The Letters of Robert Frost to Louis Untermeyer

Robert Lee Frost (1874–1963) was an American poet. Born in San Francisco, he farmed unsuccessfully in New Hampshire, but combined it with teaching and writing poetry. He sailed to England and established his reputation as the author of several books, then returned to America and won Pulitzer poetry prizes for New Hampshire, Collected Poems, A Further Range, *and* A Witness Tree.

Clark Gable

G

Frankly, my dear, I don't give a damn.

As Rhett Butler in Gone with the Wind

I am paid not to think.

Clark Gable (1901–60) was one of the great Hollywood legends for his rakish looks and charm laced with cynicism. Born in Ohio, he was an oilfield worker and lumberjack before his film bit parts of the 1920s and big break in It Happened One Night *in 1934. His last film before a heart attack was* The Misfits *with Marilyn Monroe.*

Zsa Zsa Gabor

The only place men want depth in a woman is in her décolletage.

It's wonderful to catch a man. But it's wonderful to get rid of him.

A man in love is incomplete until he is married. Then he is finished.

Zsa Zsa Gabor (1919–) was born Sari Gabor. This glamorous international lady was Miss Hungary of 1936. Married eight times, she has lived in and made films in many countries, including Lovely to Look At *(USA),* Lily *(USA),* Moulin Rouge *(GB),* Public Enemy Number One *(France) and* Diary of a Scoundrel *(USA).*

John Kenneth Galbraith

Politics is not the art of the possible. It consists in choosing between the disastrous and the unpalatable.

One can relish the varied idiocy of human action during a (financial) panic to the full, for, while it is a time of great tragedy,

G nothing is being lost but money.

The Great Crash, 1929

What is wholly mysterious in economics is not likely to be important.

Economics, Peace and Laughter

All the great leaders have had one characteristic in common; it was the willingness to confront unequivocally the major anxiety of their people in their time. This, and not much else, is the essence of leadership.

The Age of Uncertainty

John Kenneth Galbraith (1908–), US economist, was born in Canada, the son of an Ontario politician and farmer. He tutored at Harvard after his own university education and rose up the academic ladder while writing extensively on economics. He also served as US ambassador in India. He challenged economic orthodoxies particularly in The Affluent Society, *his major assessment in 1958 of American economic, social and political issues.*

Paul Getty

My formula for success? Rise early, work late, strike oil.

If all the money and property in the world were divided up equally at say, three o'clock in the afternoon, by 3.30 there would already be notable differences in the financial conditions of the recipients. . . After ninety days the difference would be staggering.

As I See It

The meek may inherit the earth — but not its mineral rights.

If you can count your money then you are not a rich man.

John Paul Getty (1892–1976), the son of a wealthy American business-man, made his first million by the age of twenty-one buying and selling oil leases. He continued buying oil shares in the 1930s depression and, with his wealth from the Getty Oil Company, bought a collection of art, furniture and tapestries for his museum in California. By the 1960s he was regarded as the world's wealthiest man but installed a pay phone for guests staying at his English mansion. His five marriages all ended in divorce. He wrote several autobiographies.

Kahlil Gibran

You give but little when you give of your possessions. It is when you give of yourself that you truly give.

The Prophet

Much of your pain is self-chosen. It is the bitter potion by which the physician within you heals your sick self.

The Prophet

In the depths of your hopes and desires lies your silent knowledge of the beyond; and like seeds dreaming beneath the snow your heart dreams of spring. Trust the dreams, for in them is hidden the gate to eternity.

The Prophet

Kahlil Gibran (1883–1931), poet and painter, is often called the Blake of the twentieth century. Born in Lebanon, he studied art in Paris and Arabic literature in Beirut before migrating to New York in 1912. His best-known work, The Prophet, *has remained in print since 1923 through the power of its mysticism. It was the first of a trilogy with* The Garden of the Prophet *and* The Death of the Prophet.

W.S. Gilbert

When I was a lad I served a term
As office-boy to an Attorney's firm.
I cleaned the windows and I swept the floor,

G And I polished up the handle of the big front door.

HMS Pinafore

The House of Peers throughout the war,
Did nothing in particular
   And did it very well.

Iolanthe

Husband twice as old as wife,
Argues ill for married life.

Princess Ida

Awaiting the sensation of a short, sharp shock
From a cheap and chippy chopper on a big black block.

The Mikado

Life's a pudding full of plums.

The Gondoliers

When in the House MPs divide
If they've a brain and cerebellum, too,
They've got to leave that brain outside,
And vote just as their leaders tell 'em to.

Iolanthe

Sir William Schwenk Gilbert (1836–1911), the British humorist and dramatist, collaborated with Sir Arthur Sullivan in a great series of comic-operas, the popularity of them being due as much to Gilbert's lyrics as to Sullivan's music. Unfortunately, the personal relationship between the two men became cool, and the partnership broke down owing to temperamental incompatability.

Johann Wolfgang von Goethe

It is not doing the thing we like to do, but liking the thing we have to do, that makes life blessed.

Give me the benefit of your convictions if you have any;

but keep your doubts to yourself, for I have enough of my own.

To rule is easy, to govern difficult.

Everything has been thought of before, but the problem is to think of it again.

Proverbs in Prose

If you inquire what the people are like here, I must answer 'The same as everywhere!'

Die Leiden des Jungen Werthers

Johann Wolfgang Von Goethe (1749–1832), the German poet and man of letters, statesman and natural philosopher, discovered his poetic vocation while studying law at Leipzig. He met Herder at Strasbourg and became leader of the Storm and Stress movement. Later he moved to Weimar and entered the service of Duke Karl August. The first part of his Faust *appeared in 1808, but the second part was not published until 1831.*

Oliver Goldsmith

When lovely woman stoops to folly,
And finds too late that men betray,
What charm can soothe her melancholy,
What art can wash her guilt away?

The Vicar of Wakefield

Handsome is as handsome does.

The Vicar of Wakefield

Women and music should never be dated.

She Stoops to Conquer

All men have their faults; too much modesty is his.

A man he was to all the country dear,
And passing rich with forty pounds a year.

The Deserted Village

I love everything that's old; old friends, old times, old manners,
old books, old wines.

She Stoops to Conquer

Oliver Goldsmith (1728–74) was born in Ireland, the son of a clergyman. He was educated at Trinity College, Dublin, then went to Edinburgh to study medicine. Later he went abroad and wandered through France, Switzerland and Italy, then returned to England and wrote his History of England *and* Animated Nature. *Upon meeting Johnson he became a member of his 'Club', established his reputation with his poem* The Traveller, *and followed it with some collected essays,* The Vicar of Wakefield, The Deserted Village *and* She Stoops to Conquer.

Samuel Goldwyn

Anyone who visits a psychiatrist wants his head examined.

A verbal contract isn't worth the paper it's written on.

The most important thing in acting is honesty. Once you've learned to fake that, you're in.

In two words: im possible.

Why should people go out to see bad films when they can stay at home and see bad television?

The reason so many people showed up at Louis B. Mayer's funeral was because they wanted to make sure he was dead.

Going to call him William? What kind of a name is that? Every Tom, Dick and Harry's called William. Why don't you call him Bill?

Yes, my wife's hands are very beautiful. I'm going to have a bust made of them.

If you can't give me your word of honour, will you give me your promise?

Samuel Goldwyn (1882–1974) was born of Jewish parents in Warsaw. As a Pole with an unpronounceable name, he arrived in the United States, and an immigration official named him 'Goldfish'. Eventually he realised the trick that had been played on him and changed it to Goldwyn. He founded the Goldwyn Pictures Corporation which later became the Metro-Goldwyn-Mayer Company in 1925. He is particularly famed for his witty sayings or 'Goldwynisms'.

Mikhail Sergeyevich Gorbachov

We have made huge breaches in the walls of the Cold War fortress. . . The era of nuclear disarmament has begun.
After Moscow Summit, 1.6.1988

We are learning democracy and glasnost, learning to argue and conduct a debate, to tell one another the truth.
Speech to 19th All-Union Party Conference in Moscow, 29.6.1988

We have no right to permit perestroika to founder on the rocks of dogmatism and conservatism, on anyone's prejudices and personal ambitions. What is at stake is the country's future, the future of socialism.
Speech to 19th All-Union Party Conference in Moscow, 29.6.1988

G *Mikhail Sergeyevich Gorbachov (1931–), Soviet political leader, came from peasant origins. He studied law and agronomy, then worked as a Communist Party official, rising to the Supreme Soviet in 1970 and then the Central Committee. He became the youngest member of the Politburo in 1980, midway through a seven-year term as Agriculture Minister. His overall leadership from 1985 has been marked by profound political, social and economic reforms and readiness to negotiate with America in a series of summits.*

Kenneth Grahame

Believe me, my young friend, there is *nothing* – absolutely nothing – half so much worth doing as simply messing about in boats.

The Wind in the Willows

The clever men at Oxford
Know all that there is to be knowed.
But they none of them know one half as much
As intelligent Mr. Toad.

The Wind in the Willows

Kenneth Grahame (1859–1932) was born in Edinburgh, son of an advocate, and worked at the Bank of England from 1878 to 1908. His early volumes of sketches of childhood – The Golden Age *and* Dream Days *– were followed by his masterpiece* The Wind in the Willows, *an animal fantasy originally created for his little son. It became a successful stage play in A.A. Milne's dramatisation as* Toad of Toad Hall.

Thomas Gray

The curfew tolls the knell of parting day,
The lowing herd winds slowly o'er the lea,
The ploughman homeward plods his weary way,
And leaves the world to darkness and to me.

Elegy written in a Country Churchyard

Full many a flower is born to blush unseen,
And waste its sweetness on the desert air.

Elegy written in a Country Churchyard

Not all that tempts your wand'ring eyes
And heedless hearts, is lawful prize;
Not all that glisters, gold.

Ode on the Death of a Favourite Cat

. . . Where ignorance is bliss
'Tis folly to be wise.

Ode on a Distant Prospect of Eton College

Thomas Gray (1716–71) was born in London. At Eton he formed a close friendship with Horace Walpole and together they went on a tour of France and Italy. Upon his return, Gray lived again in London, but visited his mother and sister as Stoke Poges. For some time he wrote poems which appeared anonymously in Dodsley's Miscellany, *but in 1750 he wrote the now famous* Elegy written in a Country Churchyard. *The location was presumed to be Stoke Poges.*

Joyce Grenfell

If I should go before the rest of you
Break not a flower nor inscribe a stone,
Nor when I'm gone speak in a Sunday voice
But be the usual selves that I have known.

Quoted in 'Radio Times', 1.1.1981

Weep if you must,
Parting is hell,
But life goes on,
So sing as well.

Quoted in 'Radio Times', 1.1.1981

Joyce Grenfell (1910–79), comedienne, film-star, expert at writing and speaking monologues, panellist on Joseph Cooper's 'Face the Music' programmes – Joyce Grenfell was all this and much more. Her books very quickly became bestsellers, and gave the fascinating story of her life.

Sir Edward Grey

The lamps are going out all over Europe; we shall not see them lit again in our lifetime.

71

G *Sir Edward Grey (1st Viscount of Fallodon, 1862–1933), British diplomat, was the eldest son of Captain George Henry Grey. He was educated at Winchester and Balliol College, Oxford. A member of parliament for thirty-one years, he was Foreign Secretary from 1905 to 1916 and spoke his fateful words when the German invasion of Belgium caused Britain's declaration of war in 1914.*

François Guizot

Do not be afraid of enthusiasm. You need it. You can do nothing effectually without it.

François Pierre Guillaume Guizot (1787–1874) was a French statesman and historian. Born at Nîmes, he was a Protestant and from 1812 to 1830 was professor of history at the Sorbonne. He became Foreign Minister in 1840 and for almost a decade controlled the government although he was named Prime Minister only in 1847.

Nubar Sarkis Gulbenkian

The best number for a dinner party is two — myself and a damn good chef.

Nubar Sarkis Gulbenkian (1896–1972) was the son of Armenian-born oil magnate Calouste Sarkis Gulbenkian, who was named Mr Five Per Cent for his holding in the Anglo-Iranian Petroleum Company. He worked for thirty years with his father and although most of the fortune was left to a philanthropic trust, enough remained for the son to be a colourful figure on the London social scene.

Joseph Hall

Moderation is the silken string running through the pearl chain of all virtues.

Christian Moderation, Introduction

Joseph Hall (1574–1656) was Bishop of Exeter and Norwich. Educated at Ashby-de-la-Zouch and Emmanuel College, Cambridge, he published some satires which were attacked by Marston in 1601. He became chaplain to Henry, Prince of Wales, and chaplain to Lord Doncaster in France; also he accompanied James I to Scotland. Impeached and imprisoned in 1642, he had his episcopal revenues sequestered in 1643 and was expelled from his palace in 1647.

Oscar Hammerstein II

A sudden beam of moonlight, or a thrush you have just heard, or a girl you have just kissed, or a beautiful view through your study window is seldom the source of an urge to put words on paper. Such pleasant experiences are likely to obstruct and delay a writer's work.

Oscar Hammerstein II (1895–1960) was an immensely successful American lyricist who wrote many stage musicals, usually with Richard Rodgers, his old college classmate. Together they achieved fame with such shows as The King and I, South Pacific *and* The Sound of Music, *and are well remembered for such songs as* Oh What a Beautiful Morning *and* Younger than Springtime. *Hammerstein's grandfather was Oscar Hammerstein I, an operatic impressario.*

Thomas Hardy

This is the weather the cuckoo likes,
And so do I:
When showers betumble the chestnut spikes
And nestlings fly;
And the little brown nightingale bills his best,
And they sit outside at the 'Traveller's Rest'.

Weathers

H The chronic melancholy which is taking hold of the civilized races with the decline of belief in a beneficent power.

Tess of the D'Urbervilles

I leant upon a coppice gate
When Frost was spectre-gray,
And Winter's dregs made desolate
The weakening eye of day.

The Darkling Thrush

Don't you go believing in sayings, Picotee; they are all made by men, for their advantage.

The Hand of Ethelberta

Thomas Hardy (1840–1928) became widely known and acclaimed as the Wessex author. Born at Bockhampton near Dorchester, he wrote Far From the Madding Crowd *and* Under the Greenwood Tree *there before moving away and writing* The Return of the Native, The Mayor of Casterbridge *and others, including his famous* Tess of the D'Urbervilles. *He also wrote many poems.*

Joel Chandler Harris

Lazy fokes' stummucks don't get tired.

Plantation Proverbs

Licker talks mighty loud w'en it gits loose fum de jug.

Plantation Proverbs

Joel Chandler Harris (1848–1908), the American writer, was born in Georgia and first published his Uncle Remus *stories in the Atlanta* Constitution *which he edited from 1890 to 1905. The tales were written in Negro dialect and gained worldwide popularity. His autobiography* On the Plantation *was published in 1892.*

Minnie Louise Haskins

And I said to the man who stood at the gate of the year: 'Give me a light that I may tread safely into the unknown'. And he replied: 'Go out into the darkness and put your hand into the hand

74

of God. That shall be to you better than light and safer than a **H**
known way.'
From 'God Knows', quoted by King George VI in his Christmas broadcast 1939

Minnie Louise Haskins (1875–1957), English author and educator, went to Clarendon College, Clifton, the London School of Economics and the University of London. She taught in England and India, and supervised women factory workers during World War I. She lectured at the LSE until 1939.

William Hazlitt

Give me the clear blue sky over my head, and the green turf beneath my feet, a winding road before me, and a three hours' march to dinner.

Table Talk

The rule for travelling abroad is to take our common sense with us, and leave our prejudices behind.

Table Talk

William Hazlitt (1778–1830), English essayist and critic, dabbled in portrait painting, but took to writing on the advice of Coleridge. He then went to London where he contributed to the press and various magazines. He became famous for, amongst other works, Table Talk *and* The Spirit of the Age.

Edward Heath

If politicians lived on praise and thanks, they'd be forced into some other line of business.

30.9.1973

I have told the country before that capitalism has its unacceptable face. If you want to see the acceptable face of capitalism, go out to an oil-rig in the North Sea.

24.2.1974

H *Edward Heath (1916–), English politician, was leader of the Conservative Party from 1965–75, and Prime Minister for four of those years. His unswerving faith in European unity was rewarded in 1972 by Britain's successful application for entry into the European Economic Community. His premiership from 1970 to 1974 was marked by bitter confrontation with the unions. In the contest for the leadership of the Conservative Party held in February 1975, he was defeated in the first ballot by Margaret Thatcher and did not contest the second.*

Felicia Dorothea Hemans

The boy stood on the burning deck
Whence all but he had fled;
The flame that lit the battle's wreck
Shone round him o'er the dead.

Casabianca

Oh! What a crowded world one moment may contain!

The Last Constantine

Felicia Dorothea Hemans (1793–1835), a British poet, was born in Liverpool. She published many volumes of sentimental verse which attained great popularity, but her best-known poem is Casabianca.

William Ernest Henley

It matters not how strait the gate,
How charged with punishments the scroll,
I am the master of my fate:
I am the captain of my soul.

Echoes: Invictus. In Memoriam of R.T. Hamilton Bruce

William Ernest Henley (1849–1903), English poet, was born at Gloucester. Tuberculosis and the subsequent amputation of a left leg left him crippled from boyhood. He wrote much verse, criticism and miscellaneous journalism, and was closely associated with Stevenson, with whom he wrote Deacon Brodie *and other plays.*

Robert Herrick

I sing of brooks, of blossoms, birds and bowers;
Of April, May, of June and July flowers

Hesperides: The Argument of His Book

Gather ye rosebuds while ye may
Old Time is still a-flying. . .

Hesperides: To the Virgins

Robert Herrick (1591–1674) was born in Cheapside, the son of a London goldsmith. On return from university, he became friendly with dramatist Ben Jonson and his literary set. In 1629 he became vicar of Dean Prior, near Totnes, and in 1648 published Hesperides, *which was a collection of sacred and pastoral poetry of unrivalled lyric quality.*

Paul Hindemith

People who make music together cannot be enemies, at least not while the music lasts.

A Composer's World

Paul Hindemith (1895–1963) was a German composer. A fine viola player, he led the Frankfurt Opera Orchestra at twenty, and taught composition at the Berlin Hochschule for Music from 1927 to 1933, when the modernity of his Philharmonic Concerto *led to a Nazi ban. In 1939 he went to America where he taught at Yale and in 1952 he became professor of musical theory at Zurich.*

Alfred Hitchcock

Suspense is a matter of knowledge. If a bomb unexpectedly goes off in a film – that's surprise. But if the audience knows a bomb will go off in five minutes, and the hero on screen doesn't know it – that's suspense.

Alfred Hitchcock (1899–1981) was a British film director and a master of suspense. His notable films include The Thirty-Nine Steps, Rebecca, Rope, Strangers on a Train, Rear Window, Vertigo, Psycho *and* The Birds.

Oliver Wendell Holmes

Fate tried to conceal him by naming him Smith.

Poems of the Class of '29

H Man has his will — but woman has her way.

The Autocrat of the Breakfast Table

It is the province of knowledge to speak and it is the privilege of wisdom to listen.

The Poet at the Breakfast Table

A moment's insight is sometimes worth a life's experience.

The Professor at the Breakfast Table

Oliver Wendell Holmes (1809–94) was an American author and physician. Born at Cambridge, Massachusetts, he became professor of anatomy at Dartmouth and later at Harvard. Later still with Lowell he founded the Atlantic Monthly *and wrote humorous essays collected in the* Breakfast Table *series.*

Thomas Hood

Never go to France
Unless you know the lingo.
If you do, like me,
You will repent, by jingo.

French and English

Thomas Hood (1799–1845) was a British poet. Born in London, he entered journalism and edited periodicals which included Hood's Magazine. *Best known for his comic verse, he also wrote serious poems such as* Song of the Shirt *and* Bridge of Sighs.

Horace

He who has begun his task has half done it.

Epistles

If you do not know how to live aright, make way for those who do. . . It is time for you to leave the scene.

Epistles

What shall be to-morrow, think not of asking. Each day that Fortune gives you, be it what it may, set down for gain.

Odes

Never despair (Nil desperandum).

Quintus Horatius Flaccus Horace (65–8BC), the Roman poet, was born at Venusia in Apulia and was present on the losing side at the battle of Philippi, but obtained his pardon and returned to Rome. He was given a Sabine farm and then wrote poems which included Satires, Odes, Epistles *and the* Ars Poetica.

Sir Fred Hoyle

Outer space isn't remote at all. It's only an hour's drive away if your car could go straight upward.

It is the true nature of mankind to learn from mistakes, not from example.

Into Deepest Space

Sir Fred Hoyle (1915–), the British astronomer, was educated at Cambridge and became Plumian professor of astronomy and experimental philosophy there in 1958. He became famous for his radio talks and science fiction. He taught at Cambridge 1945–72 and at Cornell 1972–78. He theorised the universe as in a 'steady state' of continuous growth, without beginning or end.

Victor Hugo

Common-sense is in spite of, not the result of, education.

Victor Marie Hugo (1802–85) was a French poet, novelist and dramatist. Born at Besançon, the son of one of Napoleon's generals, he established himself as the leader of French Romanticism with the verse play Hernani. *Later plays included* Lucrece Borgia. *In 1851 he was banished for opposing Louis Napoleon's coup d'état and settled in Guernsey, but on the fall of the Empire in 1870 he returned to France and became a senator.*

T.H. Huxley

The rung of a ladder was never meant to rest upon, but only to hold a man's foot long enough to enable him to put the other somewhat higher.

H If a little knowledge is dangerous, where is the man who has so much as to be out of danger?

Science and Culture

I asserted — and I repeat — that Man has no reason to be ashamed of having an ape for his grandfather.

Speech to the British Association at Oxford, 30.6.1860

Thomas Henry Huxley (1825–95) was a British scientist, humanist and agnostic thinker. Born at Ealing, he graduated in medicine and for several years was surgeon to HMS Rattlesnake *on a surveying expedition in the South Seas. Following the publication of* The Origin of Species *in 1859, he won fame as 'Darwin's bulldog', and for many years was the most prominent and popular champion of evolution.*

Jerome K. Jerome

Love is like the measles; we all have to go through it.
> *Idle Thoughts of an Idle Fellow, On Being in Love*

I like work, it fascinates me. I can sit and look at it for hours. I love to keep it by me: the idea of getting rid of it nearly breaks my heart.
> *Three Men in a Boat*

Jerome Klapka Jerome (1859–1927), after being educated in London, became a clerk and a teacher. In 1885 he published On the Stage and Off, *then made his name with* Three Men in a Boat. *This was followed by* Idle Thoughts of an Idle Fellow *and several novels. Jerome K. Jerome wrote many plays, the best known of which is probably* The Passing of the Third Floor Back.

Samuel Johnson

Prepare for death if here at night you roam,
And sign your will before you sup from home.
> *London*

I am not yet so lost in lexicography, as to forget that words are the daughters of earth, and that things are the sons of heaven.
> *Preface: Dictionary of the English Language*

A man, Sir, should keep his friendship in constant repair.
> *Letter to Lord Chesterfield, 1755*

Depend upon it, Sir, when a man knows he is to be hanged in a fortnight, it concentrates his mind wonderfully.
> *Letter to Lord Chesterfield*

Kindness is generally reciprocal; we are desirous of pleasing others because we receive pleasure from them.

Adversity is the state in which a man most easily becomes acquainted with himself, being especially free from admirers then.

Of all the griefs that harass the distress'd,

J Sure the most bitter is a scornful jest.

London

It is a man's own fault, it is from want of use, if his mind grows torpid in old age.

Life of Johnson

When two Englishmen meet, their first talk is of the weather.

The Idler

Samuel Johnson (1709–84) was an English lexicographer, author and critic. Born in Lichfield, he was educated at Lichfield Grammar School and Pembroke College, Oxford. He entered the service of Edward Cave the printer and in 1747 issued the 'plan' of his Dictionary *for Lord Chesterfield's consideration but it was not published until 1775. Short of money, he continued to write essays until a crown pension enabled him to spend more time with his literary circle of friends in Fleet Street, including David Garrick and his biographer, James Boswell.*

Joseph Joubert

What is left of human wisdom after age has purified it may be the best we have.

One should choose for a wife only a woman one would choose for a friend if she were a man.

A clever talk between two men is a unison: between a man and a woman it is harmony; we come away satisfied by one, enchanted by the other.

He who has no poetry in himself will find poetry in nothing.

We must respect the past and mistrust the present if we are to safeguard the future.

It is better to turn over a question without deciding it than to decide it without turning it over.

The evening of life comes bearing its own lamp. **J**

Joseph Joubert (1754–1824), French moralist, studied and taught at Toulouse and witnessed the revolution at first hand in Paris. He was Napoleon's inspector general of education. He is famous for his posthumously published work Pensées, Essais Maximes *and* Correspondance.

K Yousuf Karsh

Great men are often lonely. But perhaps that loneliness is part of their ability to create. Character, like a photograph, develops in darkness.

Yousuf Karsh (1908–), the Canadian photographer, was born in Armenia. He made use of strong highlights and shadows, and in 1933 opened his own studio in Ottawa. His 'bull-dog' portrait of Churchill in World War II brought him world fame.

John Keats

Seasons of mists and mellow fruitfulness,
Close bosom-friend of the maturing sun.

To Autumn

To bend with apples the moss'd cottage-trees,
And fill all fruit with ripeness to the core.

To Autumn

A thing of beauty is a joy forever:
Its loveliness increases.

Endymion

I cannot see what flowers are at my feet,
Nor what soft incense hangs upon the boughs.

To a Nightingale

'Beauty is truth, truth beauty,' – that is all
Ye know on earth, and all ye need to know.

On a Grecian Urn

Life is but a day;
A fragile dewdrop on its perilous way
From a tree's summit.

Sleep and Poetry

John Keats (1795–1821) was the son of a livery-stable keeper in Lon- **K**
don. He acquired a knowledge of Latin and history, and some French,
was apprenticed to a surgeon and became a student at Guy's Hospital.
However he soon abandoned medicine for poetry and was at first not
very successful. Later he wrote Endymion, The Eve of St. Agnes,
La Belle Dame sans Merci *and the unfinished* Eve of St. Mark.
About the same time he wrote his great odes On a Grecian Urn, To a
Nightingale *and* To Autumn, *as well as odes* On Melancholy, On
Indolence *and* To Psyche.

Helen Keller

Security does not exist in nature, nor do the children of men
as a whole experience it. Avoiding danger is no safer in the
long run than exposure. Life is either a daring adventure or
nothing.

On Security

With my three trusty guides, touch, smell and taste, I make
many excursions into the borderland of experience. . . Nature
accommodates itself to every man's necessity. If the eye is
maimed, so that it does not see the beauteous face of the day,
the touch becomes more poignant and discriminating. Nature
proceeds through practice to strengthen and augment the remaining senses.

Life with Three Senses, The World I Live In

When we do the best that we can, we never know what miracle is
wrought in our life or in the life of another.

Helen Adams Keller (1880–1968) was an American author who
became famous because of her great triumph over adversity. At
only nineteen months old she suffered an illness through which
she lost the senses of sight and hearing, and consequently became
dumb. After a painful period of frustration she was helped by the
skill and patience of Anne Sullivan Macy, who taught her how to
speak. Under Anne's expert guidance Helen Keller graduated with
honours at Radcliffe College in 1904, and later published several
books. Her first meeting with her teacher was described in William

K *Gibson's play* The Miracle Worker *(1959) which was made into a film in 1962.*

John Fitzgerald Kennedy

Let every nation know, whether it wishes us well or ill, that we shall pay any price, bear any burden, meet any hardship, support any friend, oppose any foe to assure the survival and the success of liberty.

Inaugural address, 20.1.1961

And so, my fellow Americans, ask not what your country can do for you; ask what you can do for your country.

Inaugural address, 20.1.1961

If we cannot now end our differences, at least we can help make the world safe for diversity.

Speech at American University, Washington, 10.6.1963

All free men, wherever they may live, are citizens of Berlin. And therefore, as a free man, I take pride in the words *Ich bin ein Berliner.*

Speech in West Berlin, 26.6.1963

John Fitzgerald Kennedy (1917–63), son of American banker Joseph Kennedy, was assassinated in Dallas in his third year as President. He was the youngest and first Catholic president in America's history and had promised a New Frontier of social justice and aid to under-developed nations. After the Cuban missile crisis, he signed the nuclear test ban treaty with Russia. Educated at Harvard and the London School of Economics, he commanded a torpedo boat in World War II, became a member of Congress in 1947 and the Senate in 1952.

Lord Kilmuir

When the ruins of Pompeii were uncovered, dice were found. It is a sad commentary on the unvarying conditions of human nature that some of the dice were loaded.

Sayings of the Week

Lord Kilmuir (David Patrick Maxwell Fife, 1900–67), British law- **K**
yer and Conservative politician, was called to the Bar in 1922. He
became an MP in 1935, Solicitor-General from 1942–5 and Attorney
General in 1945 during the Churchill governments. At the Nuremberg
trials he was deputy to Sir Hartley Shawcross and for most of the time
conducted the British prosecution. He was Home Secretary from 1951
to 1954 and Lord Chancellor from 1954 to 1962. In 1954 he was created
Viscount and in 1962 Earl.

Martin Luther King

I have a dream that one day on the red hills of Georgia,
the sons of former slaves and the sons of former slave-owners
will be able to sit down together at the table of brother-
hood.
Speech at Civil Rights March on Washington, 28.8.1963

I have a dream that my four little children will one day
live in a nation where they will not be judged by the
colour of their skin, but by the content of their character.
Speech at Civil Rights March on Washington, 28.8.1963

Injustice anywhere is a threat to justice everywhere.
Letter from Birmingham, Alabama Jail, 1963

I just want to do God's will. And he's allowed me to go to
the mountain. And I've looked over, and I've seen the promised
land. . . So I'm happy tonight. I'm not worried about anything.
I'm not fearing any man.
Speech at Birmingham, Alabama, 3.4.1968, the evening before his
assassination

K *Martin Luther King (1929–68) was an eloquent black Baptist minister who, from the middle 1950s until his assassination in April 1968, led the first mass civil rights movement in United States history. He achieved world-wide recognition when he was awarded the 1964 Nobel Prize for Peace for his application of the principle of non-violent resistance – patterned after India's Mahatma Gandhi – in the struggle for racial equality in America.*

Rudyard Kipling

Oh, East is East, and West is West, and never the twain shall meet,
Till Earth and Sky stand presently at God's great Judgment Seat;
But there is neither East nor West, Border, nor Breed nor Birth,
When two strong men stand face to face, though they come from the ends of the earth.

The Ballad of East and West

The female of the species is more deadly than the male.

The Female of the Species

If you can keep your head when all about you
Are losing theirs and blaming it on you,
If you can trust yourself when all men doubt
   you. . .
If you can dream — and not make dreams your master. . .
Yours is the Earth and everything that's in it,
And — which is more — you'll be a Man, my son!

If

On the road to Mandalay
Where the flyin' fishes play,
An' the dawn comes up like thunder outer
China 'crost the Bay!

Mandalay

For it's Tommy this, an' Tommy that, an' 'Chuck 'im
   out, the brute!'
But it's 'saviour of 'is country' when the guns begin
   to shoot.

Tommy

Rudyard Kipling (1865–1936) was the son of John Lockwood **K**
Kipling, the illustrator of Beast and Man in India. *He was born in
Bombay, educated in England and worked as a journalist in colonial
India between 1882 and 1889. His fame rests largely on his short sto-
ries which dealt with India, the sea, the jungle and its beasts, the army
and the navy. Kipling is best known for his two* Jungle Books, Kim,
The Just-So Stories, Puck of Pook's Hill *and* Stalky and Co. *and
he was awarded the Nobel Prize for Literature in 1907.*

Arthur Koestler

God seems to have left the receiver off the hook and time is running out.

The Ghost in the Machine

Murder within the species on an individual or collective scale is a
phenomenon unknown in the whole animal kingdom, except for
man and a few varieties of ants and rats.

Quoted in the Observer, 1968

The limitations of our biological equipment may condemn us to
the role of Peeping Toms at the keyhole of eternity.

The Roots of Coincidence

The most persistent sound reverberating through man's history
is the beating of war drums.

Janus: A Summing Up

*Arthur Koestler (1905–83), Hungarian-born writer and philosopher,
studied in Vienna. In his varied life he travelled the world as foreign
correspondent and reported on the Spanish civil war. He was one of
the first left-wing intellectuals to denounce Stalin. Imprisoned after
the fall of France, he escaped in 1940 to Britain where he settled and
became a British citizen. He wrote many novels and non-fiction about
those areas which science finds difficult to explain, like creativity and
parancrmal phenomena. He and his wife took their lives when he became ill.*

L La Bruyère

Modesty is to merit what shadow is to the figures in a picture; it gives accent and strength.

Women run to extremes: they are either better or worse than men.

Every vice falsely resembles some virtue, and it always takes advantage of the resemblance.

There is no trade in the world so toilsome as that of pursuing fame; life is over before the main part of your work has begun.

There are but three events which concern mankind; birth, life, and death. All know nothing of their birth, all submit to die, and many forget to live.

Jean de la Bruyère (1645–96), French essayist, was born in Paris, studied law, took a post in the Revenue office, and in 1684 entered the service of the house of Condé. His Caractères *(satirical portraits of contemporaries) made him many enemies.*

La Rochefoucauld

If we cannot find peace within ourselves, it is useless to look for it elsewhere.

Passion often turns the cleverest man into an idiot and the greatest blockhead into someone clever.

It takes greater character to handle good fortune than bad.

Self-interest blinds some people and sharpens the eye-sight of others.

To establish yourself in the world, do all you can to seem established already.

François, Duc de la Rochefoucauld (1613–80) was born in Paris, became a soldier and took part in the wars of the Fronde. His later years were divided between the Court and literary society. He is best known for his work Réflexions, Sentences et Maximes Morales *(1665).*

Emma Lazarus

Give me your tired, your poor,
Your huddled masses yearning to be free,
The wretched refuse of your teeming shore,
Send these, the homeless, tempest-tossed, to me;
I lift my lamp beside the golden door.

Lines inscribed on the Statue of Liberty

Emma Lazarus (1849–87), an American poet, essayist and philanthropist, was born in New York City. She published a number of works, including Alide; An Episode of Goethe's Life *in 1874. She championed oppressed Jews during persecution in Russia, and wrote* Songs of a Semite.

Stephen Leacock

Many a man in love with a dimple makes the mistake of marrying the whole girl.

Writing is not hard. Just get paper and pencil, sit down and write it as it occurs to you. The writing is easy – it's the occurring that's hard.

Stephen Leacock (1869–1944), a British humorous writer born in Hampshire, lived in Canada from 1876 and became head of the department of economics at McGill University, Montreal, from 1908 until 1936. He published works on politics and economics, and studies of Mark Twain and Dickens, but is best known for his humorous writings. These include Literary Lapses, Nonsense Novels *and* Frenzied Fiction.

Edward Lear

'How pleasant to know Mr. Lear!'
Who has written such volumes of stuff!
Some think him ill-tempered and queer,

L But a few think him pleasant enough.

Nonsense Songs: Preface

The Owl and the Pussy-Cat went to sea
In a beautiful pea-green boat.
They took some honey, and plenty of money,
Wrapped up in a five-pound note.

The Owl and the Pussy-Cat

There was an Old Man with a beard,
Who said: 'It is just as I feared!
Two owls and a hen,
Four larks and a wren
Have all built their nests in my beard.'

On the coast of Coromandel
Where the early pumpkins blow,
In the middle of the woods
Lived the Yonghy-Bonghy-Bò.
Two old chairs, and half a candle –
One old jug without a handle –
These were all his worldy goods.

Nonsense Songs: The Courtship of the Yonghy-Bonghy-Bò

Edward Lear (1812–88), the British artist and humorist, first attracted attention with his paintings of birds, but later turned to painting landscapes. He travelled to Italy, Greece, Egypt and India and published books on his travels with his own illustrations. He published his Book of Nonsense *in 1846, which he illustrated himself, and popularised the limerick.*

C.S. Lewis

Friendship is born at the moment when one person says to another, 'What! You too? I thought I was the only one.'

A sensible human once said. 'She's the sort of woman who lives for others — you can tell the others by their hunted expression.'

The Screwtape Letters

Clive Staples Lewis (1898–1963) was a British scholar. From **L**
*1954 to 1963 he was professor of Medieval and Renaissance
English at Cambridge, and his books include the remarkable medieval study* The Allegory of Love *and the science fiction* Out
of the Silent Planet. *He also wrote some essays in popular theol-
ogy, the autobiographical* Surprised by Joy, *and a number of books
for children.*

Abraham Lincoln

In giving freedom to the slave we assure freedom to the
free, — honourable alike in what we give and what we pre-
serve.

Annual Message to Congress, 1862

Fourscore and seven years ago our fathers brought forth on this
continent, a new nation, conceived in Liberty, and dedicated to
the proposition that all men are created equal.

Address at Gettysburg, 19.11.1863

We here highly resolve that these dead shall not have died in vain;
that this nation, under God, shall have a new birth of freedom,
and that government of the people, by the people, for the people,
shall not perish from the earth.

Address at Gettysburg, 1863

I claim not to have controlled events, but confess plainly that
events have controlled me.

Letter to A.G. Hodges, 1864

'A house divided against itself cannot stand.' I believe this
government cannot endure permanently, half slave and half
free.

Speech, 16.6.1858

With malice towards none; with charity for all; with firmness in
the right, as God gives us to see the right, let us strive on to finish
the work we are in; to bind up the nation's wounds; to care for him
who shall have borne the battle, and for his widow and his orphan
– to do all which may achieve and cherish a just and lasting peace

L among ourselves and with all nations.

Second Inaugural Address, 1865

I don't know who my grandfather was, I am much more concerned to know what his grandson will be.

Abraham Lincoln (1809–65) was the sixteenth President of the USA. Born in a Kentucky log cabin, he was almost entirely self-educated but qualified as a lawyer. Entering politics, he sat first as a Whig, then joined the new Republican Party in 1856, and became President on a minority vote in 1860. Between his election and his inauguration seven slave states seceded from the Union, and these were followed by four more. Civil War soon followed and his presidency was wholly occupied by it. In 1863 his proclamation freed slaves in the Confederate territory. Five days after Robert E. Lee's surrender Lincoln was assassinated by a Confederate fanatic.

David Lloyd George

You cannot feed the hungry on statistics.

Speech 1904

Don't be afraid to take a big step if one is indicated. You can't cross a chasm in two small jumps.

David Lloyd George (1863–1945), British Liberal statesman and Prime Minister 1916–22, was champion of the under-privileged and introduced old-age pensions. Born in Manchester, the son of a Welsh teacher, he became an MP, making his reputation as an eloquent Welsh Nationalist. World War I brought him fame as the dominating figure in the Cabinet - he was Prime Minister of the coalition government in 1916 – and after the war he was among those primarily responsible for the Versailles peace settlement.

Christopher Logue

When all else fails
Try Wales.

To a Friend in Search of Rural Seclusion

Christopher Logue (1926–), Portsmouth-born English writer and **L**
translator, has written plays, songs and poetry, and contributed to the
satirical magazine Private Eye. *His anthologies include rhymes and*
comic verse for children. He wrote the play The Lilywhite Boys *and*
the screenplay for Savage Messiah.

Henry Wadsworth Longfellow

Lives of great men all remind us
We can make our lives sublime,
And, departing, leave behind us
Footprints in the sands of time.

A Psalm of Life

Let us, then, be up and doing,
With a heart for any fate;
Still achieving, still pursuing,
Learn to labour and to wait.

A Psalm of Life

Ships that pass in the night, and speak each other in passing;
Only a signal shown and a distant voice in the darkness;
So on the ocean of life we pass and speak one another,
Only a look and a voice; then darkness again and a silence.

Tales of a Wayside Inn, The Theologian's Tale

Then the little Hiawatha
Learned of every bird its language,
Learned their names and all their secrets,
How they built their nests in Summer,
Where they hid themselves in Winter,
Talked with them whene'er he met them,
Called them 'Hiawatha's chickens'.

Hiawatha's Childhood

Silently one by one, in the infinite meadows of heaven,
Blossomed the lovely stars, the forget-me-nots of the angels.

Evangeline

The heights of great men reached and kept
Were not attained by sudden flight,

L But they, while their compassion slept,
Were toiling upward in the night.

The Ladder of Saint Augustine

And the night shall be filled with music,
And the cares that infest the day,
Shall fold their tents like the Arabs,
And as silently steal away.

The Day is Done

Under the spreading chestnut tree
The village smithy stands;
The smith, a mighty man is he,
With large and sinewy hands.

The Village Blacksmith

Henry Wadsworth Longfellow (1807–82), the American poet, published his volume of poems Voices in the Night *in 1839 and* Ballads and Other Poems *in 1841. These were soon followed by* Poems on Slavery, Hiawatha *(1855),* The Courtship of Miles Standish *and* Tales of a Wayside Inn.

Anita Loos

Kissing your hand may make you feel very very good, but a diamond and sapphire bracelet lasts for ever.

Gentlemen Prefer Blondes

So this gentleman said a girl with brains ought to do something else with them besides think.

Gentlemen Prefer Blondes

Anita Loos (1893–1981), the American humorist, collaborated with her husband in writing motion-picture scenarios, and was author of Gentlemen Prefer Blondes *(1925) and* But Gentlemen Marry Brunettes *(1928).*

Samuel Lover

When once the itch of literature comes over a man, nothing can cure it but the scratching of a pen.

Handy Andy

Samuel Lover (1797–1868) was born in Dublin and became a **L**
painter of miniatures, but in 1835 he settled in London and conquered
society by singing his own compositions. These he published as Songs
and Ballads, *but he is also remembered for his humorous novels* Rory
O'More *and* Handy Andy.

Edward George Bulwer-Lytton

Beneath the rule of men entirely great
The pen is mightier than the sword.

Richelieu

Revolutions are not made with rose-water.

The Parisians

Edward George Bulwer-Lytton (1803–73), 1st Baron Lytton, was
born in London. His father was a soldier and his mother a member
of the old family of Lytton. He published his first poems in 1820, and
later his novels followed every turn of the public taste. he put his energy
into literature and politics instead of into his unhappy marriage. After
succeeding to the Knebworth estates in 1843, he concentrated less on
historical romance and more on politics, where his work — including
a spell as Colonial Secretary — was rewarded by a peerage.

M Thomas Macaulay

Then out spake brave Horatius,
The Captain of the Gate:
'To every man upon this earth
Death cometh soon or late.

And how can man die better
Than facing fearful odds,
For the ashes of his fathers,
And the temples of his gods?'

Lays of Ancient Rome

The Puritan hated bear-baiting, not because it gave pain to the bear, but because it gave pleasure to the spectators.

History of England

Nothing is so useless as a general maxim.

On Machiavelli

There were gentlemen and there were seamen in the navy of Charles the Second. But the seamen were not gentlemen; and the gentlemen were not seamen.

History of England

Thomas Babington Macaulay (1800–59), British historian, essayist, poet and politician, was born in Leicester and educated at Cambridge. In 1826 he was called to the Bar. In 1825 he published in the Edinburgh Review *his essay on Milton, and this was followed in the next twenty years by numerous historical and critical essays. Macaulay entered Parliament as a Whig (Liberal) in 1830 and advocated parliamentary reform and the abolition of slavery. He also spent several years in India as a member of the Supreme Council, and was mainly responsible for the Indian penal code.*

Harold Macmillan

Most of our people have never had it so good. Go around the country — go to the industrial towns, go to the farms — and you will see a state of prosperity such as we have never had in my lifetime, or indeed ever in the history of this country.

Speech, 20.7.1957

The wind of change is blowing through the (African) continent. Whether we like it or not, this growth of national consciousness is a political fact.

Speech to South African Parliament, 3.2.1960

Harold Macmillan (1894–1986), created Earl of Stockton in 1984, was Prime Minister 1957–63 and in later years the elder statesman of British politics. A grandson of the founder of the Macmillan publishing company, he first entered Parliament in 1924, combining politics with publishing. In 1951 he became Housing Minister, followed by Defence, the Foreign Ministry, the Exchequer and finally the premiership. He resigned due to ill health following the Profumo callgirl scandal which embarrassed his government.

Marie-Antoinette

Let them eat cake.

Marie-Antoinette (1755–93), Austrian-born consort of King Louis XVI of France, was claimed by her enemies to have said this when told the people had no bread. Her extravagent behaviour and opposition to reform fuelled the unrest that sparked the French Revolution, in which both she and her husband lost their heads.

Christopher Marlowe

Was this the face that launch'd a thousand ships,
And burnt the topless towers of Ilium?
Sweet Helen, make me immortal with a kiss.

Faustus

M O thou art fairer than the evening air,
Clad in the beauty of a thousand stars.

Faustus

Whoever loved, that loved not at first sight?

Hero and Leander

Christopher Marlowe (1564–93), English dramatist and poet, was born in Canterbury, the son of a shoemaker. He was educated at Cambridge and obtained a degree. From there he went to London, where he associated with Shakespeare and other writers of the time. Soon he attached himself to the Earl of Nottingham's theatrical company, which produced most of his plays. It has been suggested that Christopher Marlowe was part author of Shakespeare's Titus Andronicus *and that he also wrote parts of* Henry VI *and* Edward III.

Andrew Marvell

Had we but world enough, and time,
This coyness, lady, were no crime. . .
But at my back I always hear
Time's winged chariot hurrying near;
And yonder before us lie
Deserts of vast eternity.

To His Coy Mistress

He nothing common did or mean
Upon that memorable scene.
But with his keener eye
The axe's edge did try.

On the Execution of King Charles I

Andrew Marvell (1621–78), English poet and politician, was the son of a Yorkshire clergyman. He travelled Europe in his early twenties, then worked as a tutor, writing some of his best poetry. He entered Parliament in 1659. He grew to become an admirer of Oliver Cromwell and, after the restoration of King Charles II in 1660, wrote political satire.

Groucho Marx

I never forget a face, but I'll make an exception in your case.

There's one way to find out if a man is honest — ask him. If he says yes, you know he's a crook.

I find television very educating. Every time somebody turns on the set I go into the other room and read a book.

Groucho (Julius) Marx (1895–1977) was one of five sons of German migrants. All five appeared on Broadway as the Marx Brothers and four continued together in a series of 1930s Hollywood comedies. The film characters with Groucho (Julius) were Harpo (Arthur), Chico (Leonard) and Zeppo (Herbert). Groucho, who specialised in puns and insults, also hosted a TV quiz show You Bet Your Life *for fifteen years until 1962.*

Karl Marx

The history of all hitherto existing society is the history of class struggles.

The Communist Manifesto

The workers have nothing to lose but their chains. They have a world to gain. Workers of the world, unite!

The Communist Manifesto

Religion. . .is the opium of the people.

Critique of the Hegelian Philosophy of Right

Karl Marx (1818–83), father of modern communism, was born in Germany, the son of a Jewish lawyer. He switched his studies from law to philosophy. His attacks on the German goverment caused closure of a journal he edited. He was also expelled from Paris and Brussels. In London he produced the Communist Manifesto *with Frederich Engels in 1848. With the financial support of Engels, his life-long friend, he researched economics in the British Museum reading room. His major dialectic thesis was* Das Kapital, *which provided the intellectual basis for most socialist parties.*

John Masefield

I must down to the seas again, to the lonely sea and the sky,
And all I ask is a tall ship and a star to steer her by –
And the wheel's kick and the wind's song and the white sail's
   shaking,

101

M And a grey mist on the sea's face, and a grey dawn breaking.

Sea Fever

I must down to the seas again, for the call of the running tide
Is a wild call and a clear call that may not be denied.

Sea Fever

Dirty British coaster with a salt-caked smoke stack,
Butting through the Channel in the mad March days,
With a cargo of Tyne coal,
Road rail, pig lead,
Firewood, ironware, and cheap tin trays.

Cargoes

John Masefield (1878–1967) was born in Ledbury, Herefordshire, ran away to sea, and while in the USA worked as a barman in New York. He returned to England and worked on the Manchester Guardian, *then settled in London and attracted notice for some volumes of poetry. Fame came with his verse narrative* The Everlasting Mercy, *and he was later appointed poet laureate.*

William Somerset Maugham

I'll give you my opinion of the human race. . .Their heart's in the right place, but their head is a thoroughly inefficient organ.

The Summing Up

Life is too short to do anything for oneself that one can pay others to do for one.

The Summing Up

People ask you for criticism, but they only want praise.

Of Human Bondage

Somerset Maugham (1874–1965), British novelist and playwright, **M**
was born in Paris and read philosophy and literature at Heidelberg.
He then qualified as a surgeon in London and his medical work in the
slums featured in his autobiographical novel Of Human Bondage.
Freed from medicine by a legacy, he began writing plays before serving
both as doctor and secret agent in World War I. His voyage to Tahiti
provided material for The Moon and Sixpence. *He was also master*
of the short story, many of them based on his travels in Asia. He lived
in the South of France from 1928.

André Maurois

The difficult part of an argument is not to defend one's opinion
but rather to know it.

In England there is only silence or scandal.

André Maurois (1885–1967) was the pseudonym of the French author
Emile Herzog. In World War I he was attached to the British Army,
and his essays Les Silences du Colonel Bramble *(1918) give humor-*
ously sympathetic observations on the British character.

Joyce McKinney

I loved Kirk so much I would have skied down Mount Everest in
the nude with a carnation up my nose.

In court, 1977

Joyce McKinney (1950–), a former Wyoming beauty queen, rose to
brief international notoriety when charged in an English court with
kidnapping Kirk Anderson, an American Mormon missionary, and
chaining him to a bed in a country hideaway. In her defence, she
made this remarkable declaration of love. She later skipped bail and
Britain, evading trial by her disappearance.

Yehudi Menuhin

Music creates order out of chaos.

Quoted in Sunday Times, 1976

Above other arts, music can be possessed without knowledge.
Being an expression largely of the subconscious, it has its direct

M routes from whatever is in our guts, minds and spirits, without need of a detour through the classroom.

Unfinished Journey

Yehudi Menuhin (1916–) is an American violinist. Born of Russian-Jewish parentage, he gave his first concert at the age of eight. Two years later he made a tour of Europe, dazzling the critics by his maturity and freshness of approach. Retiring for a period of intensive study, he then achieved such a depth of interpretation, particularly in the Elgar and Beethoven concertos, that he soon became known as one of the world's greatest players. In 1963 he founded the Yehudi Menuhin School at Stoke D'Abernon, Surrey, a boarding school for talented musicians, which is the only one of its kind outside Russia.

George Meredith

I expect that Woman will be the last thing civilised by man.

The Ordeal of Richard Feverel

I've studied men from my topsy-turvy
Close, and, I reckon, rather true.
Some are fine fellows: some, right scurvy:
Most a dash between the two.

Juggling Jerry

Kissing don't last. Cooking do!

The Ordeal of Richard Feverel

Lovely are the curves of the white owl sweeping,
Wavy in the dusk lit by one large star.

Love in the Valley

George Meredith (1828–1909) was a British novelist and poet. Born in Portsmouth, he was educated in Germany and then articled to a London solicitor but he soon entered journalism. He published Poems *and* The Shaving of Shagpat *but his first realistic psychological novel,* The Ordeal of Richard Feverel, *was followed by a number of others including* The Egoist, Diana of the Crossways *and* The Amazing Marriage. *Later he wrote* Modern Love *and* Poems and Lyrics.

Alice Meynell

Thou art like silence unperplexed,
A secret and a mystery

Between one footfall and the next.

To The Beloved

Flocks of the memories of the day draw near
The dovecot doors of sleep.

At Night

Alice Christiana Gertrude Meynell (1847–1922) was a British poet and essayist whose essays include Rhythm of Life *and* Second Person Singular. *Her youngest son, Sir Francis Meynell, founded the Nonsuch Press and was knighted in 1946.*

Michelangelo

The hand that follows intellect can achieve.

Michelangelo Buonarroti (1745–1564) was an Italian painter, sculptor, architect and poet. His early works express the humanistic ideals of the High Renaissance, but his later work shows the instability of Church and State after the Reformation and the Sack of Rome. Michelangelo's first patron was Lorenzo de Medici, and he worked for the Medici family for much of his life. Pope Julius II commissioned him to carve his tomb, but interrupted the work by telling him to paint the ceiling of the Sistine Chapel.

George Mikes

An Englishman, even if he is alone, forms an orderly queue of one.

How to be an Alien

Continental people have sex lives; the English have hot-water-bottles.

How to be an Alien

The New Poor of yester-year are fighting a losing battle. To remain poor needs the utmost skill and ingenuity.

How to be Inimitable

M *George Mikes (1912–87) was born in Budapest and lived in exile in England, for many years as President of PEN. He was theatrical critic of Budapest newspapers for some time. He published a number of humorous books including* How to be an Alien, How to Scrape Skies, Wisdom for Others, Milk and Honey, Down with Everybody *and* Shakespeare and Myself.

Alan Alexander Milne

I am a Bear of Very Little Brain, and long words Bother me.

Winnie the Pooh

They're changing guard at Buckingham Palace—
Christopher Robin went down with Alice.
Alice is marrying one of the guard.
'A soldier's life is terrible hard,'
Says Alice.

When We Were Very Young

Alan Alexander Milne (1882–1956), English writer, was born in London and educated at Trinity College, Cambridge, where he edited an under-graduate magazine. He joined the humorous magazine Punch *in 1906 and remained there until the outbreak of World War I. His children's stories and poems were originally written for his son named Christopher Robin.* Winnie the Pooh, Now We Are Six, The House at Pooh Corner *and* The Dover Road *were all published in the 1920s. He dramatized Kenneth Grahame's* Wind in the Willows *as* Toad of Toad Hall *in 1929.*

John Milton

The mind is its own place, and in itself
Can make a Heav'n of Hell, a Hell of Heav'n.

Paradise Lost

Long is the way,
And hard, that out of hell leads up to light.

Paradise Lost

To live a life half dead, a living death.

Samson Agonistes

Calm of mind, all passion spent.

Samson Agonistes

When I consider how my light is spent,
E're half my days, in this dark world and wide,
And that one Talent which is death to hide
Lodg'd with me useless, though my Soul more bent
To serve therewith my Maker, and present
My true account.

Sonnet On his Blindness

He that has light within his own clear breast
May sit i' th' centre and enjoy bright day;
But he that hides a dark soul and foul thoughts
Benighted walks under the midday sun;
Himself is his own dungeon.

Comus

Fame is the spur that the clear spirit doth raise
(That last infirmity of noble mind)
To scorn delights, and live laborious days.

Lycidas

Sport that wrinkled Care derides,
And Laughter holding both his sides.
Come and trip it as ye go
On the light fantastic toe.

L'Allegro

John Milton (1604–74), English poet, was the son of a scrivener and composer of music. He was educated at St Paul's School and Christ's College, Cambridge. After leaving Cambridge he lived with his father at Horton in Buckinghamshire, and whilst there he read the classics. This education and his love of Italian Renaissance poetry prepared the ground for his epic poems. He was a parliamentarian and, after the execution of King Charles I, he was appointed Latin secretary to the newly-formed Council of State. He became blind but retained his post as Latin secretary until the Restoration, when he was arrested and fined. He was soon released, but lost the greater part of his fortune.

Marilyn Monroe

I've been on a calendar, but never on time.

Look, 1962

M I had the radio on.

When asked by a reporter if she had anything on at the time

Marilyn Monroe (1926–62), born Norma Jean Baker and brought up in a succession of foster homes, became Hollywood's sex symbol. She was typecast as the dumb blonde in many films, especially Gentlemen Prefer Blondes. *But she also played comedy as in* Some Like It Hot *and had a serious role in* The Misfits, *written by her third husband, playwright Arthur Miller. She died of barbiturate poisoning.*

Montaigne

When I play with my cat, who knows if I am more of a pastime to her than she is to me?

There is no torture that a woman would not endure to enhance her beauty.

The greatest thing in the world is to know how to be sufficient unto oneself.

The strength of any plan depends on timing.

We are all made up of fragments, so shapelessly and strangely assembled that every moment, every piece plays its own game. There is as much difference between us and ourselves as between us and others.

Let us give Nature a chance; she knows her business better than we do.

A learned man is not learned in all things; but an able man is able in all, even in ignorance.

No man is exempt from saying silly things. The misfortune is to say them seriously.

Dying is the greatest task we have to do, but practice can give us no assistance.

Michel Eyquem de Montaigne (1533–92), the French essayist, was **M**
born at the Château de Montaigne near Bordeaux. He studied law
and became a councillor of Bordeaux. For a time he frequented the
Court of Francis II but eventually retired to his estates and wrote sev-
eral volumes of Essays *revealing his insatiable intellectual curiosity.*
He became preoccupied with the subject of death after the premature
death of his friend La Boétie.

Baron de Montesquieu

Civility costs nothing and buys everything.

Baron Charles Louis de Secondat Montesquieu (1689–1755) was a
French philosophical historian. Born near Bordeaux, he became ad-
viser to the Bordeaux government in 1714 but, after the success of his
Lettres persanes *in 1721, he adopted a literary career.*

Desmond Morris

We are, to put it mildly, in a mess, and there is a strong chance
that we shall have exterminated ourselves by the end of the century. Our only consolation will have to be that, as a species, we
have had an exciting term of office.

The Naked Ape

Clearly, then, the city is not a concrete jungle, it is a human zoo.
The Human Zoo

Desmond Morris (1928–), British anthropologist, is best known for his
studies of Homo Sapiens as a species through his books The Naked Ape
(1967) and The Human Zoo *(1969). Educated at Birmingham Uni-*
versity and Oxford's Magdalen College, he continued his research into
animal behaviour at Oxford, then headed a film unit at the Zoological
Society of London and for eight years was its Curator of Mammals.
His many other books include Manwatching, The Soccer Tribe *and*
works on pandas and snakes.

William Morris

Forget six counties overhung with smoke,
Forget the snorting steam and piston stroke,
Forget the spreading of the hideous town;

M Think rather of the pack-horse on the down,
And dream of London small and white and clean,
The clear Thames bordered by its gardens green.

Prologue to The Earthly Paradise

William Morris (1834–96), the British poet and craftsman, was born at Walthamstow and was educated at Marlborough School and Exeter College, Oxford, where he formed a lasting friendship with Edward Burne-Jones the painter and designer and was influenced by Ruskin and Rossetti. The Earthly Paradise was written in 1868–70, but a visit to Iceland in 1871 inspired his greatest poem Sigurd the Volsung and his translations of the Sagas.

Napoléon I

England is a nation of shopkeepers.

From the sublime to the ridiculous is but a step.

Referring to the retreat from Moscow, 1812

An army marches on its stomach.

Napoléon Bonaparte (1769–1821), Emperor of France, was born in Corsica, educated at various military schools, and rose up the French revolutionary forces to become army commander in 1795. The following year he married the widowed Joséphine de Beauharnais. He conquered northern Italy and then Egypt, but his fleet was destroyed by Nelson in the 1798 battle of the Nile. He came to power in a coup in 1799 and established a vast empire with himself declared as emperor in 1804. A remarkable administrator, he reorganized France's government, code of law, roads and ports. Long invincible as a general, he abdicated in 1814 when his foreign enemies, including the Duke of Wellington, advanced against him. He was sent to Elba but escaped, and for a hundred days was emperor again until defeated at Waterloo in 1815 by the Prussians and British. He was exiled to the Atlantic island of St Helena.

Ogden Nash

One man's remorse is another's reminiscence.

Tell me, O Octopus, I begs,
Is those things arms, or is they legs?

Candy
Is dandy,
But liquor
Is quicker.

Reflections on Ice-breaking

Oh, what a tangled web do parents weave

N When they think that their children are naive.

Baby, What Makes the Sky Blue?

One would be in less danger
From the wiles of a stranger
If one's own kin and kith
Were more fun to be with.

Family Court

Women would rather be right than reasonable.

Frailty, Thy Name Is a Misnomer

The truth I do not stretch or shove
When I state the dog is full of love.
I've also proved, by actual test
A wet dog is the lovingest.

Everyone But Thee and Me, The Dog

If you should happen after dark
To find yourself in Central Park,
Ignore the paths that beckon you
And hurry, hurry to the zoo.
And creep into the tiger's lair.
Frankly, you'll be safer there.

Everyone But Thee and Me, City Greenery

Ogden Nash (1902–71) was born in Rye, New York. This American poet was noted for his humorous verse with its unconventional rhymes and quietly puncturing satire. His numerous collections of poems included You Can't Get There from Here *(1957) and* Untold Adventures of Santa Claus *(1965).*

Horatio Nelson

I have only one eye – I have a right to be blind sometimes. I really do not see the signal.

At the Battle of Copenhagen, Southey's 'Life of Nelson'

England expects that every man will do his duty.

His Signal at Trafalgar

Thank God, I have done my duty.

At Trafalgar

Kiss me, Hardy.

His disputed dying words to his flag-captain at Trafalgar

Horatio, Viscount Nelson (1758–1805), British naval commander in the Napoleonic wars, was born at Burnham Thorpe, Norfolk, and entered the navy in 1770. He saw continuous service until 1787, but returned to the navy in 1793 and fought in the Mediterranean. While commanding the Naval Bridge at Calvi, Corsica, he lost his right eye. As Commodore in the Mediterranean he was responsible for the victory of Cape St Vincent in 1797. He lost his right arm in an engagement at Santa Cruz, and won an overwhelming victory over the French in Aboukir Bay. Soon after this he met Emma Hamilton, whose husband was ambassador in Naples. Their relationship lasted to his death. In 1801 he won another victory at Copenhagen, and in October 1805, now a Viscount and Commander-in-Chief, he sailed to his last victory, the Battle of Trafalgar, during which he was fatally wounded in the spine.

Sir Henry John Newbolt

Take my drum to England, hang et by the shore,
Strike et when your powder's runnin' low –

The Island Race: Drake's Drum

To set the cause above renown,
To love the game beyond the prize,
To honour, while you strike him down,
The foe that comes with fearless eyes.

The Island Race: Clifton Chapel

There's a breathless hush in the Close to-night –
Ten to make and the match to win –
A bumping pitch and a blinding light,

N An hour to play and the last man in.

The Island Race: Vitaî Lampada

Sir Henry John Newbolt (1862–1938) was a British poet and barrister. He was also an authority on naval matters and wrote The Year of Trafalgar *(1905) and* A Naval History of the War, 1914–18 *(1920). His* Songs of the Sea *and* Songs of the Fleet *were set to music by Sir Charles Villiers Stanford, the Irish composer. Knighted in 1915, he became official naval historian eight years later.*

Sir Isaac Newton

I do not know what I may appear to the world, but to myself I seem to have been only like a boy playing on the sea-shore and diverting myself in now and then finding a smoother pebble or a prettier shell than ordinary, whilst the great ocean of truth lay all undiscovered before me.

Brewsters' Memoirs of Newton

If I have seen farther, it is by standing upon the shoulders of giants.

Sir Isaac Newton (1642–1727), British physicist and mathematician, was educated at Grantham Grammar School and Trinity College, Cambridge. At the age of twenty-three, he worked out his idea of gravitation reputedly after seeing an apple fall in his garden. He backed his conceptions of the universe with mathematical tools like the binomial theorem and the differential calculus. He published his New Theory about Light and Colours, *and later (with Halley) his greatest work* Philosophiae Naturalis Principia Mathematica *(1687), in which he sought to explain all physical phenomena by a few generalised laws.*

Beverley Nichols

Why this passion for shaking people out of ruts? I am devoted to ruts. Moreover, most of the people who are in ruts are much nicer, and much happier, than the people who are not. Ruts are

the wise old wrinkles that civilization has traced on the earth's
ancient face.

The Gift of a Home

Beverley Nichols (1901–83), prolific British author and composer, was educated at Marlborough College and Balliol College, Oxford. For a time he was President of the Oxford Union and Editor of Isis *and he was also founder and editor of the Oxford* Outlook. *Amongst other works he published his autobiography,* Twenty-Five, *in 1926.*

Friedrich Nietzsche

Is man only a blunder of God or God only a blunder of man?

Woman was God's second blunder.

Friedrich Wilhelm Nietzsche (1844–1900), the German philosopher, showed such promise before his own graduation that he was appointed Professor of Philology at Basle University at twenty-five. The son of a Lutheran pastor, he turned against religion and became convinced Christianity was worthless. His theme of a superman was developed in Thus Spake Zarathustra, *used long after his death by the Nazis to develop their theories of nationalism and race. Nietzsche was insane the last eleven years of his life.*

Richard Nixon

Let no one expect to make his fortune – or his reputation – by selling America short.

22.8.1971

There can be no whitewash at the White House.

Before the culmination of the Watergate crisis in 1974

I let down my friends. I let down my country. I let down our system of government.

8.5.1977

N *Richard Milhous Nixon (1913–) became Republican President of the United States for two terms of office (1969–74) and during that time he negotiated the withdrawal of American troops from South Vietnam and began a process of reconciliation with China and détente with the Soviet Union. At home the Watergate scandal — an illegal break-in at the Democratic campaign headquarters and subsequent cover-up by the Nixon camp — brought disgrace and an end to his presidency.*

Denis Norden

Middle age is when, wherever you go on holiday, you pack a sweater.

If all the world's a stage, and all the men and women merely players, where do all the audiences come from?

Denis Norden (1922–) is a British writer and comedian, educated at Craven Park School. He served in the RAF from 1942–45 and afterwards became staff writer in a variety agency. He first teamed up with Frank Muir in 1947, and is a very experienced and successful radio and television broadcaster.

Kathleen Norris

From birth to eighteen a girl needs good parents. From eighteen to thirty-five she needs good looks. From thirty-five to fifty-five a woman needs personality; and from fifty-five on the old lady needs cash.

Kathleen Norris (1880–1966) was born in San Francisco, California, and spent her early years in Mill Valley, a small mountain village in California. she was the daughter of James Alden Thompson and Josephine Moroney and married Charles Gilman Norris who died in 1945. Kathleen became librarian, social worker and writer, producing many novels. Her last one was Family Gathering, *published in 1959.*

Alfred Noyes

The wind was a torrent of darkness among the gusty trees,
The moon was a ghostly galleon tossed upon cloudy seas,
The road was a ribbon of moonlight over the purple moor,

And the highwayman came riding –
The highwayman came riding, up to the old inn door.

The Highwayman

Go down to Kew in lilac-time (it isn't far from London)
And you shall wander hand in hand with love in summer's
wonderland.

The Barrel Organ

Alfred Noyes (1880–1958), British poet, was educated at Oxford and later became professor of modern English literature at Princeton University. His best-known poems include The Highwayman *and* The Barrel Organ, *but he also wrote* Drake, The Torch Bearers *and* The Accusing Ghost, *which was an attempt to clear the name of Roger Casement.*

Awake! for Morning in the Bowl of Night
Has flung the Stone that puts the Stars to Flight
And Lo! the Hunter of the East has caught
The Sultan's Turret in a Noose of Light.

Rubáiyát

Here with a Loaf of Bread beneath the bough,
A Flask of Wine, A Book of Verse – and Thou
Beside me singing in the Wilderness –
And Wilderness is Paradise enow.

Rubáiyát

'Tis all a Chequer-board of Nights and Days
Where Destiny with Men for Pieces plays:
Hither and thither moves, and mates, and slays,
And one by one back in the Closet Lays.

Rubáiyát

The Moving Finger writes: and, having writ,
Moves on: nor all thy Piety nor Wit
Shall lure it back to cancel half a Line,
Nor all thy Tears wash out a Word of it.

Rubáiyát

Ah, my Beloved, fill the Cup that clears
Today of past Regrets and Future Fears:
Tomorrow! – Why, Tomorrow I may be
Myself with Yesterday's Seven Thousand Years.

Rubáiyát

Ah, make the most of what we yet may spend,
Before we too into Dust descend;
Dust into Dust, and under Dust, to lie,
Sans Wine, sans Song, sans Singer, and – sans End!

Rubáiyát

Ah, Moon of my Delight who know'st no wane,

The Moon of Heav'n is rising once again:
How oft thereafter rising shall she look
Through this same Garden, after me – in vain!

Rubáiyát

Omar Khayyám was an eleventh-century astronomer and poet whose name 'Khayyám' means 'tent-maker'. He was born at Naishapur in Khorassan in the latter half of the century. The stanzas contain the poet's meditations on the mysteries of existence, and his counsel to drink and make merry while life lasts. His work was translated into the English poetic version by Edward FitzGerald in the nineteenth century.

George Orwell

I sometimes think that the price of liberty is not so much eternal vigilance as eternal dirt.

The Road to Wigan Pier

Big Brother is watching you.

1984

If you want a picture of the future, imagine a boot stamping on a human face — for ever.

1984

George Orwell (1903–1950) was the pseudonym of Eric Blair, Eton-educated English novelist whose early writing concerned his stint with the police in Burma and chosen poverty in London and Paris. He was wounded fighting on the Republican side in the Spanish Civil War. His theme of poverty in The Road to Wigan Pier (1937) was followed by the evils of Stalinism in Animal Farm (1946) and three years later he produced 1984, his vision of a totalitarian state which he feared as mankind's future.

Ovid

Take rest; a field that has rested gives a beautiful crop.

To be loved, be lovable.

O There is no such thing as pure pleasure; some anxiety always goes with it.

Ovid (43BC–AD17) was a Roman poet, whose full name was Publius Ovidius Naso. He was born at Sulmo and studied rhetoric in Rome in preparation for a legal career but soon turned to literature. In AD8 he was banished by Augustus to Tomi on the Black Sea, where he died. This punishment was supposedly for his immoral Ars Amatoria but was probably due to some connection with Julia, the profligate daughter of Augustus.

John Owen

God and the doctor we alike adore
But only when in danger, not before;
The danger o'er, both are alike requited,
God is forgotten, and the doctor slighted.

Epigrams

Times change, and we change with them too.

Epigrams

John Owen (1560?–1622), the Welsh epigrammist, was a master of Latin idioms and the author of a number of shrewd and pointed epigrams.

Ignacz Jean Paderewski

Piano playing is more difficult than statesmanship. It is harder to awake emotions in ivory keys than it is in human beings.

Ignacz Jean Paderewski (1860–1941) was a Polish pianist, composer and statesman. The son of a Polish patriot, he gained European and American fame after his debut in Vienna in 1887 and became a noted exponent of Chopin. During World War I he raised money in America for the relief of Polish war victims and organised the Polish army in France. In 1919 as Prime Minister he represented the newly independent Poland at the Peace Conference.

Dorothy Parker

Careful, son, of the cursed two –
Either one is a dangerous pet;
Natural history proves it true –
Women and elephants never forget.
Ballade of Unfortunate Mammals

Men seldom make passes
At girls who wear glasses.

Congratulations: we all knew you had it in you.
Telegram to a friend who had just had a baby

She ran the whole gamut of her emotions, from A to B.
Remark about an actress

Byron and Shelley and Keats
Were a trio of lyrical treats.
The forehead of Shelley was cluttered with curls,
And Keats never was a descendant of earls,

P And Byron walked out with a number of girls. . .
The Lives and Times of Keats, Shelley and Byron

Four be the things I'd be better without,
Love, curiosity, freckles and doubt.

Inventory

O, it is then, Utopian
To hope that I may meet a man
Who'll not relate, in accents suave,
The tales of girls he used to have?

De Profundis

That woman speaks eighteen languages, and she can't say 'no' in any of them.

Dorothy Parker (1893–1967) was an American writer, born in the West End of New Jersey into the famous Rothschild family. She became Mrs Alan Campbell, and wrote verse and a number of short stories, quickly establishing a reputation for an acid wit and scathing comment.

Blaise Pascal

The heart has its reasons which reason knows nothing of.

Imagination is the deceitful part of man, a mistress of error and falsity who cheats us the more because she does not cheat us always.

If you want people to think well of you, do not speak well of yourself.

Can anything be more ridiculous than that a man should have the right to kill me because he lives on the other side of the water and

122

because his ruler has a quarrel with mine?

Blaise Pascal (1623–62), the French philosopher, was a mathematical prodigy, showing as a child his father's brilliance for figures. Later he investigated the laws governing the weight of air, the equilibrium of liquids, the hydraulic press, the infinitesimal calculus, and the mathematical theory of probability. In 1654 he went to live at a religious community where his sister had already become a nun.

James Payn

I had never had a piece of toast
Particularly long and wide,
But fell upon the sanded floor
And always on the buttered side.

Chambers's Journal

James Payn (1830–98), the English novelist, was editor of Chambers' Journal *from 1859 to 1874, and of* The Cornhill Magazine *from 1883 to 1896. He was also author of a number of novels including* Lost Sir Massingberd.

Samuel Pepys

This morning came home my fine camlet cloak, with gold buttons, and a silk suit, which cost me much money, and I pray God to make me able to pay for it.

Diary, 1 July 1660

I went out to Charing Cross, to see Major-general Harrison hanged, drawn and quartered; which was done there, he looking as cheerful as any man could do in that condition.

Diary, 13 Oct 1660

P As happy a man as any in the world, for the whole world seems to smile upon me.

Diary, 31 Oct 1662

My wife, who, poor wretch, is troubled with her lonely life.

Diary, 19 Dec 1662

Went to hear Mrs Turner's daughter . . . play on the harpischon; but, Lord! it was enough to make any man sick to hear her; yet was I forced to commend her highly.

Diary, 1 May 1663

Saw a wedding in the church . . . and strange to say what delight we married people have to see these poor fools decoyed into our condition.

Diary, 25 Dec 1665

Samuel Pepys (1633–1703) the British diarist, was born in London. He entered the navy office in 1660, shortly after beginning his diary. Appointed secretary to the Admiralty in 1672, he was later imprisoned, with loss of office, on suspicion of being connected with the Popish Plot. Reinstated in 1684 but finally deprived at the 1688 Revolution, he retired to Clapham. Pepys' Diary was written in his own personal version of Shelton's shorthand and was not deciphered until 1825. Discontinued in 1669 because of his failing sight, it is nevertheless unrivalled for its intimacy and the graphic picture it gives of seventeenth-century English life.

Pablo Picasso

I do not seek – I find.

God is really another artist. He invented the giraffe, the elephant

and the cat. He has no real style. He just goes on trying other
things.

Pablo Ruiz Picasso (1881–1973) was a famous Spanish artist, son of art teacher José Ruiz Blasco and an Andalusian mother Maria Picasso Lopez, but he discontinued the use of the name Ruiz in 1898. Born at Malaga, he was a mature artist at ten, and at sixteen was holding his first exhibition. From 1901–4 he had his Blue Period, when he painted mystic distorted figures in blue tones; he followed this with his Rose Period, Cubism, etc. He was unique in the fertile vigour of his invention, and his exhibitions attracted a large popular following.

William Pitt

Confidence is a plant of slow growth in an aged bosom; youth the season of credulity.
Speech in House of Commons, 14.1.1766

The poorest man may in his cottage bid defiance to all the forces of the crown. It may be frail – its roof may shake – the wind may blow through it – the storm may enter – but the King of England may not enter . . .
Speech on the Excise Bill

William Pitt (1708–78), first Earl of Chatham, entered Parliament as MP for Old Sarum and gained a reputation for himself by his attacks on the Prime Minister, Sir Robert Walpole. For a time he was Paymaster-General. He helped to form the ministry which continued the war against the French (Seven Years' War), and was largely responsible for the British victories in Canada and India and on the seas. Known as Pitt the Elder, he was father of William Pitt the Younger, who became Prime Minister.

Plato

Philosophy is a longing after heavenly wisdom.

P Pleasure is the greatest incentive to evil.

Self-conquest is the greatest of victories.

Plato (c429–347BC) the Greek philosopher, was born in Athens. He had political ambitions but came under the influence of Socrates and about the year 387BC founded the Academy of Athens, an institute for the study of philosophy. Plato remained in Athens except for two visits to Syracuse in 367 and 361–60BC.

Plutarch

I don't need a friend who changes when I change and who nods when I nod; my shadow does that much better.

Plutarch (AD46–120) was born in Greece at Chacronea, lectured on philosophy at Rome and was appointed procurator of Greece by Hadrian. His Parallel Lives *consists of pairs of biographies of Greek and Roman soldiers and statesmen, followed by comparisons between the two. North's translation inspired Shakespeare's Roman plays.*

Edgar Allan Poe

On desperate seas long wont to roam
Thy hyacinth hair, thy classic face,
Thy Naiad airs, have brought me home
To the glory that was Greece
And the grandeur that was Rome.

To Helen

'Ghastly grim and ancient Raven wandering from the
   Nightly shore —
Tell me what thy lordly name is on the Night's
   Plutonian shore!'
Quoth the Raven, 'Nevermore.'

The Raven

Edgar Allan Poe (1809–49) was an American author born in Boston
but orphaned at the age of two. He was brought up by a Mr and Mrs
Allan, whose surname he used as a middle name from 1824. After a
period of poverty and alcoholism and the death of his wife, he concen-
trated on writing poems of melancholy beauty. His reputation rests on
short stories of horrific atmosphere such as The Fall of the House of
Usher, *and certain detective stories such as* The Gold Bug *and* The
Murders in the Rue Morgue *which laid the foundations of modern*
detective fiction.

Alexander Pope

Happy the man whose wish and care
A few paternal acres bound,
Content to breathe his native air,
In his own ground.

Ode on Solitude

Words are like leaves; and where they most abound,
Much fruit of sense beneath is rarely found.

An Essay on Criticism

Be not the first by whom the new are tried,
Nor yet the last to lay the old aside.

An Essay on Criticism

To err is human, to forgive, divine.

An Essay on Criticism

For fools rush in where angels fear to tread.

An Essay on Criticism

Who sees with equal eye, as God of all,
A hero perish, or a sparrow fall,
Atoms or systems into ruin hurl'd,
And now a bubble burst, and now a world.

An Essay on Man

All are but parts of one stupendous whole,
Whole body Nature is, and God the soul.

An Essay on Man

P Hope springs eternal in the human breast;
Man never is, but always to be blest.

An Essay on Man

Alexander Pope (1688–1744), English poet and satirist, was the son of a Roman Catholic linen-draper of London. A severe illness at the age of twelve ruined his health and distorted his figure, but he showed his literary skill in his Pastorals *when he was sixteen. He became known to Joseph Addison's circle and soon published his* Messiah, *which was followed by his* Rape of the Lock. *His* Ode for Music on St. Cecilia's Day *was not very successful, but he also published* Windsor Forest *which was well received. He moved from Addison's circle and became a member of the Scriblerus Club, an association which included Swift, Gay, Arbuthnot and other famous writers.*

Richard Porson

I went to Frankfort where I got drunk
With that most learn'd profesor, Brunck;
I went to Worms, and got more drunken
With that more learn'd professor, Ruhnken.

Facetiae Cantabrigienses, 1825

Richard Porson (1759–1808), a Regius profesor of Greek at Cambridge, edited four plays of Euripides. His finest single piece of criticism was his supplement to the preface to his Hecuba. *His elucidation of Greek idiom and usage and his editing of texts advanced Greek scholarship.*

Cole Porter

Night and day, you are the one,
Only you beneath the moon and under the sun.

Night and Day

It was great fun,
But it was just one of those things.

Just One of Those Things

Cole Porter (1891–1964), American songwriter, began writing songs **P**
as a student at Yale and Harvard. His Broadway musicals brightened
the 1930s depression with shows like Anything Goes. *A riding accident*
in 1937 injured both his legs but despite lingering disability, he wrote
Kiss Me Kate *in 1949 and* Can-Can, Silk Stockings *and* High Society *in the 1950s.*

Dilys Powell

Society splits into cat-lovers and dog-lovers. For years I cared
chiefly for cats. Later I came round to dogs as well – to dogs,
I mean, as sharers of bed and board. A cat is a house guest.
A dog joins the family. He makes friends for you, or at any
rate, acquaintances. People one might never have spoken to
greet one warmly; they know your dog's name when you remain
anonymous.

Animals in My Life, Sunday Times, 27.6.1976

Dilys Powell CBE (1901–) was Sunday Times *film critic from*
1939–76 and now reviews films for Punch. *She is the author of sev-*
eral books, including The Villa Ariadne.

Enoch Powell

A little nonsense now and then is not a bad thing. Where
would we politicans be if we were not allowed to talk it sometimes?

On Politics, 19.12.1965

History is littered with wars which everybody knew would never
happen.

Speech on immigration April 1968, a reference to Virgil's 'Aeneid'

You don't lead people by following them, but by saying what they
want to follow.

6.12.1970

All political lives, unless they are cut off in mid-stream at a happy
juncture, end in failure, because that is the nature of politics and
of human affairs.

P *John Enoch Powell (1912–), British politician, was educated at King Edward's School, Birmingham and Trinity College, Cambridge. He became Craven Travelling Student of 1933, Fellow of Trinity College, Cambridge, from 1934–83, and Professor of Greek in the University of Sydney, Australia, from 1937–9. Often an outspoken and controversial figure during his thirty-seven years in Parliament, Enoch Powell has held various appointments on the British General Staff, has been Parliamentary Secretary of the Ministry of Housing and Local Government, Financial Secretary to the Treasury, and Minister of Health.*

J.B. Priestley

Fountains enchant me – in the daytime, when the sunlight turns their scattered drops into diamonds; after dark when coloured lights are played on them, and the night rains emeralds, rubies, sapphires.

Essays

To travel swiftly in a closed car, as so many of us do nowadays, is to cut oneself off from the reality of the regions one passes through, perhaps from any sane reality at all. Whole leagues of countryside are only a roar and a muddle outside the windows, and villages are only like brick-coloured bubbles that we burst as we pass. Their life is temporarily as remote as the moon.

English Journey

John Boynton Priestley (1894–1984), the prolific British novelist, was born in Bradford, the son of a schoolmaster. He was educated at Trinity Hall, Cambridge, and served in World War I. He established his reputation as a novelist with The Good Companions *and later wrote* Angel Pavement, Dangerous Corner, An Inspector Calls, *and other well-known plays.*

HRH Prince Philip

It is no good shutting your eyes and saying 'British is Best' three times a day after meals, and expecting it to be so.

29.4.1956

I have been wet and frozen, and fried in the sun. I have **P**
walked for miles through fields and over hills; I have frightened
myself silly climbing to the top of rickety pigeon platforms, and
I have sat shivering on the edge of a kale field in a blizzard.

To anyone with a conventional view of pleasure, to the town-living,
comfort-loving commuter, the idea that there might be any thrill in
wildfowling or rough shooting must seem too painfully ludicrous
to be considered. . .

. . .Yet this is the stuff of natural history, this is a certain way to
arouse enthusiasm for conservation. Without this introduction I
would never have learnt about the sights and sounds of the country and the wilderness.

Published in Saturday Evening Post

*HRH Prince Philip, Duke of Edinburgh (1921–) and husband
of Queen Elizabeth II, is a grandson of George I of Greece and
a great-grandson of Queen Victoria. He was born in Corfu but
raised in England and educated at Gordonstoun and Dartmouth
Naval College. A naturalised British subject taking the surname of
Mountbatten in March 1947, he married the then Princess Elizabeth
in Westminster Abbey, having the previous day received the title
Duke of Edinburgh. In 1956 he founded the Duke of Edinburgh's
Award Scheme to encourage creative achievement among young people.*

HRH The Princess Royal

There are always people around waiting for me to put my foot in
it, just like my father.

The Aids Pandemic is a classic own goal scored by the human
race against itself.

Speech in 1988

131

P *HRH The Princess Royal (1950–), the only daughter of Queen Elizabeth II and Prince Philip, was known as Princess Anne until her mother conferred the honorary title in 1987. She was educated at Benenden in Kent and married Captain Mark Philipps in 1973, both sharing a love of horses and eventing. Between her continuing equine interests, she carries out an enormous number of public duties, especially for charities like the Save the Children Fund for which she travels to remote areas as its President.*

Matthew Prior

Be to her virtues very kind:
Be to her faults a little blind;
Let all her ways be unconfin'd:
And clap your padlock – on her mind.

An English Padlock

They never taste who always drink,
They always talk, who never think.

Upon this Passage in Scaligerana

Matthew Prior (1664–1721), English poet and diplomat, was the son of a Dorset joiner. Educated at Westminster School and St John's College, Cambridge, under the patronage of Lord Dorset, he entered the diplomatic service and played an important part in several international treaties, including Utrecht (1713), which was known as 'Matt's Peace'. On Queen Anne's death in 1714, he was impeached and imprisoned for two years. After his release a folio edition of his poems was brought out by his admirers, by which he gained the sum of four thousand guineas.

Francis Quarles

He gives me wealth, I give him all my vows;
I give him songs, he gives me length of days;
With wreaths of grace he crowns my conquering brows;
And I his temples with a crown of praise. . .

My Beloved is Mine and I am His

My soul, sit thou a patient looker-on;
Judge not the play before the play is done:
Her plot has many changes; every day
Speaks a new scene; the last act crowns the play.

Epigram

Francis Quarles (1592–1644) was a metaphysical poet. He went abroad in the suite of Princess Elizabeth, daughter of James I, on her marriage with the Elector Palatine, and wrote pamphlets in defence of Charles I, which led to the sequestration of his property. He is chiefly remembered for his Emblems, *a book of short devotional poems which was published in 1635.*

R

François Rabelais

A child is not a vase to be filled, but a fire to be lit.

Nature abhors a vacuum.

This flea which I have in mine ear.

François Rabelais (1494–1553) was a French author, born at Chinon, Touraine. He became a monk and, having studied medicine, lectured on anatomy. He wrote several great works, particularly some satirical allegories which were laced with coarseness, broad humour and philosophy.

Ronald Reagan

I don't think anyone would cheerfully want to use atomic weapons – but the enemy should go to bed every night being afraid that we might.

Remark in July 1967, during a grim period of the Vietnam War

Nations do not distrust each other because they are armed, they are armed because they distrust each other.

Speech in London, 3.6.1988

Ronald Reagan (1911–) began his career as an actor in America in the thirties, starred in fifty films, and later became well known on television. In 1967 he became Republican Governor of California. In 1968 he made a bid for the Republican presidential nomination, which was unsuccessful, but in 1980, by a landslide victory, he was elected 40th President of the USA, to succeed President Carter in that office on 20 January 1981. At sixty-nine, he was the oldest man elected to the presidency. He was re-elected in 1984. His tough anti-Soviet foreign policy mellowed into a series of disarmament summits with Soviet leader Mikhail Gorbachov before standing down in 1988.

Sir Joshua Reynolds

It is allowed on all hands, that facts, and events, however they may bind the historian, have no dominion over the poet or the painter. With us, history is made to bend and conform to this grand idea of art. . .

These arts, in their highest province, are not addressed to the gross senses; but to the desires of the mind, to that spark of divinity which we have within.

Discourses, The Aims of Art

Sir Joshua Reynolds (1723–92), the British artist, was born near Plymouth. He went to London at the age of seventeen and was apprenticed to Thomas Hudson, a mediocre portrait painter. For several yeas he was active as a portrait painter in London and Plymouth, but in 1749 he went abroad to complete his studies. After living in Rome and other Italian cities he settled in London and became the most famous portrait painter of his day and the first President of the Royal Academy.

Sir Ralph Richardson

We actors are the jockeys of literature. The dramatist writes the plays; we try to make them run.

The most precious things in speech are pauses.

Sir Ralph David Richardson (1902–83), English actor, was born in Cheltenham and had an extensive career on stage from 1921 and in films from 1933. He also achieved great success as actor-director of the Old Vic from 1944 to 1947.

La Rochefoucauld

Before strongly desiring anything, we should look carefully into the happiness of its present owner.

The love of justice in most men is simply the fear of suffering injustice.

Nothing is given so profusely as advice.

Few people know how to be old.

135

R *François, Duc de la Rochefoucauld (1613–80) was born in Paris, became a soldier and took part in the wars of the Fronde. His later years were divided between the Court and literary society. He is best known for his work* Réflexions, Sentences et Maximes Morales *(1665).*

J.D. Rockefeller

It's easy to run into debt, but hard to crawl out even at a slow walk.

John Davison Rockefeller (1839–1937) organised the Standard Oil Company of America in 1870 and substituted combination for competition, becoming immensely rich in the process. From 1890 he undertook the philanthropic distribution of his fortune, and by the end of 1927 was said to have bestowed some £100,000,000 on such purposes.

Will Rogers

It's great to be great, but it's greater to be human.

We can't all be heroes because somebody has to sit on the curb and clap as they go by.

Will Rogers (1879–1935) was an American comedian. For a time he was in the Ziegfeld Follies, but later became famous for many films, including Almost a Husband, The Gay Cabellero *and* The Strongest Man in the World.

Christina Rossetti

Better by far you should forget and smile
Than that you should remember and be sad.

Remember

Does the road wind up-hill all the way?
Yes, to the very end.
Will the day's journey take the whole long day?
From morn to night, my friend.
But is there for the night a resting-place?
A roof for when the slow, dark hours begin. . .

Up-Hill

In the bleak mid-winter
Frosty wind made moan,
Earth stood hard as iron,
Water like a stone.

Christina Georgina Rossetti (1830–94), the British poet and sister of the poet and artist Dante Gabriel Rossetti, was a devout Anglican. She produced much popular lyric and religious verse.

Gioachino Antonio Rossini

Give me a laundry list and I'll set it to music.

Gioachino Antonio Rossini (1792–1868) was an Italian composer. Born at Pesaro, his first success was the opera Tancredi *but three years later his* Il Barbiere di Siviglia *was produced at Rome. At first it was a failure. Rossini had a fertile composition period from 1815–23 during which time he produced twenty operas. After* Guillaume Tell *(1829) he gave up writing opera and spent his time in Bologna and Paris.*

Jean-Jacques Rousseau

To live is not merely to breathe, it is to act.

Man was born free, and everywhere he is in chains.

He who is slowest in making a promise is most faithful in its performance.

What wisdom can you find that is greater than kindness?

Jean-Jacques Rousseau (1712–78) was a French philosopher who was born in Geneva. He was apprenticed to a lawyer and engraver but ran away and for some time led the wandering life described in his Confessions. *Later he published* A Discourse on The Origin of Inequality *which made him famous.*

John Ruskin

To see clearly is poetry, prophesy, and religion, all in one.

R I have seen, and heard, much of Cockney impudence before now; but never expected to hear a coxcomb ask two hundred guineas for flinging a pot of paint in the public's face.

On Whistler's 'Nocturne in Black and Gold', Fors Clavigera

John Ruskin (1819–1900), English critic, was the son of James Ruskin, a partner in a wine business. In 1843 he published anonymously the first volume of the famous Modern Painters, *of which five volumes were issued over a period of seventeen years. This first volume, written when Ruskin was only twenty-four, was conceived in a mood of indignation at the artistic ignorance of England, and written in particular to defend Turner against the attacks on his paintings. Ruskin made the acquaintance of Turner in 1840 and of Millais in 1851.*

In 1849 he published his Seven Lamps of Architecture, *which dealt with the leading principles of architecture, but which was mainly a defence of Gothic as the noblest style.* The Stones of Venice, *a treatise in three volumes, was written while the production of* Modern Painters *was continuing and its purpose was to glorify Gothic architecture and expose 'the pestilent art of the Renaissance' by attacking it in its central stronghold, Venice itself.*

Bertrand Russell

What men really want is not knowledge but certainty.

Quoted in 'The Listener', 1964

Nothing is so exhausting as indecision, and nothing is so futile.

The Conquest of Happiness

Boredom is a vital problem for the moralist, since at least half the sins of mankind are caused by fear of it.

The Conquest of Happiness

If there were in the world today any large number of people who desired their own happiness more than they desired the unhappiness of others, we could have a paradise in a few years.

New York Times, 1961

Man is a credulous animal and must believe in something. In the absence of good grounds for belief, he will be satisfied with bad **R** ones.

Unpopular Essays, 1950

Real life is, to most men, a long second-best, a perpetual compromise between the ideal and the possible.

Bertrand Arthur William Russell (1872–1970), British philosopher and mathematician, was born at Trelleck, the grandson of the first Earl Russell (Lord John Russell). He was educated at Trinity College, Cambridge, where he specialised in mathematics and became a lecturer. His pacifist attitude in World War I lost him the lectureship, and he served six months in prison for an article he wrote in a pacifist journal. After the war he went to Russia, China and the USA, where he taught at many universities. Later he returned to England and wrote many books, being awarded the OM in 1949 and the Nobel Prize for literature in 1950. On the death of his brother in 1931 he succeeded to the earldom, becoming the Third Earl.

S George Sand

We cannot tear out a single page from our life, but we can throw the whole book into the fire.

Mauprat

Life is a slate where all our sins are written; from time to time we rub the sponge of repentance over it so we can begin sinning again.

There is only one happiness in life, to love and be loved.

Letter to a friend, 31.3.1832

The whole secret of the study of nature lies in learning how to use one's eyes.

Nouvelles Lettres d'un Voyageur

George Sand (1804–76) was the pseudonym of French novelist Armandine Aurore Lucile Dupin, who married young but separated from her husband and lived in Paris as a writer. Subsequent love affairs with Alfred de Musset and Chopin demonstrated her unconventionality and search for the perfect lover.

George Santayana

We live experimentally, moodily, in the dark; each generation breaks its eggshell with the same haste and assurance as the last, pecks at the same indigestible pebbles, dreams the same dreams, or others just as absurd, and if it hears anything of what former men have learnt by experience, it corrects their maxims by its first impressions.

Those who do not remember the past are condemned to relive it.

The Life of Reason

That life is worth living is the most necessary of assumptions and, were it not assumed, the most impossible of conclusions.

The Life of Reason

S

The working of great institutions is mainly the result of a vast mass of routine, petty malice, self interest, carelessness and sheer mistake. Only a residual fraction is thought.

The Crime of Galileo

George Santayana (1863–1952) was a Spanish philosopher. Born in Madrid, he graduated at Harvard where he taught the history of philosophy from 1889 to 1911. He wrote a number of books on philosophy, several volumes of poems and the novel The Last Puritan.

Jean Paul Sartre

Hell is other people.

In Camera

Life is nothing until it is lived; but it is yours to make sense of, and the value of it is nothing other than the sense you choose.

Existentialism is a Humanism

Man is not the sum of what he has but the totality of what he does not yet have, of what he might have.

Situations

Jean Paul Sartre (1905–80), French philosopher and writer, was the leading exponent of the existentialist movement. He taught philosophy before World War II, was imprisoned by the Germans, and after release worked for the French resistance and leftist political causes. He wrote many novels as well as his main philosophical treatise, Being and Nothingness. *In 1946 he founded a magazine with French writer Simone de Beauvoir, with whom he lived.*

Robert Schumann

In order to compose, all you need is to remember a tune that nobody else has thought of.

141

S *Robert Schumann (1810–56) was a German musician. Born at Zwickau, Saxony, he taught at Leipzig Conservatoire and was musical director at Düsseldorf from 1850 to 1853. As a composer he excelled in pianoforte compositions and in Lieder. His piano concerto Opus 54 and sonatas Opus 11 and 22 are particularly famous.*

Albert Schweitzer

Many women were dying in childbirth. The elders warned them never to see a doctor, that it would bring bad luck. How can I gain power over these old witches? I thought.

Then I hit on the idea of presenting each baby born at my hospital with a little bonnet and dress. By sheer bribery, my power was established, and pregnant women have flocked to the hospital ever since.

Reader's Digest, September 1980

Albert Schweitzer (1875–1965), the French theologian, was also an organist and missionary surgeon. He founded a hospital in 1913 at Lambarene, Republic of Gabon. He remained there apart from the brief intervals spent giving recitals of organ music, mainly Bach, in order to raise funds for his medical work. He was awarded the Nobel Peace Prize in 1952. He described his personal inspiration as reverence for life.

Robert Falcon Scott

We are in a desperate state, feet frozen etc. No fuel and a long way from food, but it would do your heart good to be in our tent, to hear our songs and the cheery conversation.

Farewell letter to Sir J.M. Barrie

Great God! This is an awful place.

Journal 17.1.1912 at South Pole

For God's sake look after our people.

Last entry in Journal, 29.3.1912

Had we lived, I should have had a tale to tell of the hardihood, endurance and courage of my companions which would have stirred the heart of every Englishman. These rough notes and our dead bodies must tell the tale.

Message to the public

Robert Falcon Scott (1868–1912), the British Antarctic explorer, entered the navy in 1882. Later he commanded two Antarctic expeditions, first in the Discovery *(1901–4) and then in the* Terra Nova *(1910–12). On 18 January 1912 he reached the South Pole, only to discover that the Norwegian explorer Amundsen had already been there. On the return journey he and his companions, Wilson, Oates, Bowers, and Evans, perished, trapped in their tent by a blizzard. His journal was recovered and published. His son Peter is well known as a naturalist and for his paintings of birds.*

Sir Walter Scott

Like the dew on the mountain,
Like the foam on the river,
Like the bubble on the fountain,
Thou art gone, and for ever!

The Lady of the Lake

The way was long, the wind was cold,
The Minstrel was infirm and old;
His wither'd cheek and tresses grey,
Seem'd to have known a better day.
The harp, his sole remaining joy
Was carried by an orphan boy,

S The last of all the Bards was he,
Who sung of Border chivalry.

The Lay of the Last Minstrel

But search the land of living man,
Where wilt thou find their like again.

Marmion

O what a tangled web we weave,
When first we practise to deceive.

Marmion

A miss is as good as a mile.

Journal, 31.3.1825

Sir Walter Scott (1771–1832), a Scottish poet and novelist, was born in Edinburgh and his early education was interrupted by delicate health, coupled with lameness. He attended High School and University, and at about fifteen he entered the office of his father, a Writer to the Signet and later Sheriff of Selkirkshire and Clerk of Session. Called to the Bar in 1792, Scott devoted much of his leisure to the exploration of the Border country, which inspired his Scottish ballads and poems.

Being eclipsed to a certain extent by Byron as a poet, Scott turned his attention to the novel. Waverley *was followed by* Guy Mannering, *and a number of others including* Rob Roy, The Heart of Midlothian, Tales of my Landlord, The Bride of Lammermoor *and* A Legend of Montrose. *Scott continued to write novels, but became involved in the bankruptcy of a publishing company and liable for a debt of £114,000. He shouldered the whole burden himself, and shortened his own life by his efforts to pay off the creditors, who all received full payment after his death.*

John Selden

Old friends are best. King James used to call for his old shoes; they were the easiest for his feet.

Table Talk: Friends

A King is a thing men have made for their own sakes.

Table Talk: Of a King

Preachers say, Do as I say, not as I do.

Table Talk: Preaching

John Selden (1584–1654), an English eminent lawyer, won fame as an orientalist. Reports of his utterances appeared in Table Talk *from time to time during the last twenty years of his life and were collected by his secretary, Richard Milward.*

Seneca

Never judge your neighbour until you have been in the same situation.

Travel and change of place impart new vigour to the mind.

It is often better not to see an insult than to attempt to revenge it.

If you are surprised at the number of our maladies, count your cooks.

Lucius Annaeus Seneca (died AD65), Roman philosopher, was tutor to the young Nero, and when Nero became Emperor he was one of his chief advisors. He tried to check Nero's vices. Seneca's writings include works on moral philosophy and nine tragedies in a rhetorical style. He was accused of participating in the conspiracy of Piso and was ordered to take his own life, which he did with stoic courage.

William Shakespeare

Men are April when they woo, December when they wed; maids are May when they are maids, but the sky changes when they are wives.

As You Like It

S Age cannot wither her, not custom stale
Her infinite variety.

Antony and Cleopatra

All the world's a stage,
And all the men and women merely players:
They have their exits and their entrances;
And one man in his time plays many parts.

As You Like It

Blow, blow, thou winter wind,
Thou art not so unkind
As man's ingratitude.

As You Like It

To be or not to be: that is the question:
Whether 'tis nobler in the mind to suffer
The slings and arrows of outrageous fortune,
Or to take arms against a sea of troubles,
And by opposing end them?

Hamlet

Something is rotten in the state of Denmark.

Hamlet

I must be cruel only to be kind.

Hamlet

Neither a borrower, nor a lender be;
For loan oft loses both itself and friend,
And borrowing dulls the edge of husbandry.

Hamlet

This above all: to thine own self be true,
And it must follow, as the night the day,
Thou canst not then be false to any man.

Hamlet

Cowards die many times before their deaths;
The valiant never taste of death but once.

Julius Caesar

Beware the ides of March.

Julius Caesar

The fault, dear Brutus, is not in our stars,
But in ourselves, that we are underlings.

Julius Caesar

Friends, Romans, countrymen, lend me your ears;
I come to bury Caesar, not to praise him.
The evil that men do lives after them,
The good is oft interred with their bones.

Julius Caesar

This was the most unkindest cut of all.

Julius Caesar

There is a tide in the affairs of men,
Which, taken at the flood, leads on to fortune.
Omitted, all the voyage of their life
Is bound in shallows and in misery.

Julius Caesar

So may the outward shows be least themselves.
The world is still deceived with ornament.

The Merchant of Venice

The quality of mercy is not strain'd,
It droppeth as the gentle rain from heaven
Upon the place beneath: it is twice bless'd;

S

S It blesseth him that gives and him that takes.

The Merchant of Venice

O! swear not by the moon, the inconstant moon,
That monthly changes in her circled orb,
Lest that thy love prove likewise variable.

Romeo and Juliet

Night's candles are burnt out, and jocund day
Stands on tiptoe on the misty mountain tops.

Romeo and Juliet

What's in a name? That which we call a rose
By any other name would smell as sweet.

Romeo and Juliet

O Romeo, Romeo! wherefore art thou Romeo?
Deny thy father, and refuse thy name;
Or, if thou wilt not, be but sworn my love,
And I'll no longer be a Capulet.

Romeo and Juliet

If music be the food of love, play on.

Twelfth Night

But be not afraid of greatness: some are born great, some achieve
greatness, and some have greatness thrust upon them.

Twelfth Night

Everyone can master a grief but he that has it.

Much Ado About Nothing

Full fathom five thy father lies;
Of his bones are coral made:
Those are pearls that were his eyes:

148

Nothing of him that doth fade,
But doth suffer a sea-change
Into something rich and strange.

The Tempest

If all the year were playing holidays,
To sport would be as tedious as to work.

King Henry IV Part I

This happy breed of men, this little world,
This precious stone set in the silver sea. . .
This blessed plot, this earth, this realm, this England.

Richard II

Now is the winter of our discontent
Made glorious summer by this sun of York.

Richard III

A horse! a horse! My kingdom for a horse!

Richard III

Heat not a furnace for your foe so hot
That it do singe yourself.

King Henry VIII

To gild refined gold, to paint the lily,
To throw a perfume on the violet,
To smooth the ice, or add another hue
Unto the rainbow. . .
Is wasteful and ridiculous excess.

King John

Let me not to the marriage of true minds
Admit impediments. Love is not love
Which alters when it alteration finds.

Sonnets

149

S Shall I compare thee to a summer's day?
Thou art more lovely and more temperate.
Rough winds do shake the darling buds of May.

Sonnets

William Shakespeare (1564–1616) was born at Stratford-upon-Avon and educated at the Free Grammar School. He left Stratford in about 1582 and went to London where he joined a company of players and soon became established as an actor and playwright. His plays brought him immediate fame. His output was prolific and his collected works as published today contain 37 plays, 2 long poems and 154 sonnets. The plays are divided into 17 comedies, 10 histories and 10 tragedies. He basked in the favour of Queen Elizabeth I and her successor, King James I, but eventually ceased to write and retired once again to Stratford-upon-Avon.

George Bernard Shaw

When a stupid man is doing something he is ashamed of, he always declares that it is his duty.

Caesar and Cleopatra

Do you think that the things people make fools of themselves about are any less real and true than the things they behave sensibly about?

Candida

It is easy — terribly easy — to shake a man's faith in himself. To take advantage of that to break a man's spirit is devil's work.

Candida

He who can, does. He who cannot teaches.

Man and Superman

There are two tragedies in life. One is not to get your heart's desire. The other is to get it.

Man and Superman

Home is the girl's prison and the woman's workhouse.

Man and Superman

Marriage is popular because it combines the maximum of temptation with the maximum of opportunity.

Maxims for Revolutionists

The worst sin towards our fellow creatures is not to hate them, but to be indifferent to them: that's the essence of inhumanity.

The Devil's Disciple

The British soldier can stand up to anything except the British War Office.

The Devil's Disciple

People are always blaming their circumstances for what they are. I do not believe in circumstances. The people who get on in this world are the people who get up and look for the circumstances they want, and if they cannot find them, make them.

Success covers a multitude of blunders.

If you cannot get rid of the family skeleton, you may as well make it dance.

George Bernard Shaw (1856–1950), the son of a civil servant, left Ireland and came to London, where he became a brilliant debater among the Fabians. He wrote five novels, then became a playwright and his wit met with great success. His comedy Pygmalion *was written especially for Mrs Patrick Campbell, and his letters to the actress Ellen Terry are of great interest.*

Bishop Fulton Sheen

Each of us comes into life with fists closed, set for aggressiveness and acquisition. But when we abandon life our hands are open; there is nothing on earth we need, nothing the soul can take with it.

Bishop Fulton Sheen (1895–1979) was an American Roman Catholic prelate and auxiliary bishop of New York from 1951 to 1966. He achieved widespread influence through his radio Catholic Hour *and television programmes.*

Percy Bysshe Shelley

Like winged stars the fire-flies dash and glance,
Pale in the open moonshine, but each one
Under the dark trees seems a little sun,

151

S A meteor tamed: a fixed star gone astray
From the silver regions of the Milky Way

To Maria Gisborne in England, from Italy

I wield the flail of the lashing hail
And whiten the green plains under,
And then again I dissolve it in rain,
And laugh as I pass in thunder.

The Cloud

The seed ye sow, another reaps;
The wealth ye find, another keeps;
The robes ye weave, another wears;
The arms ye forge, another bears.

Song to the Men of England

Teach me half the gladness
That thy brain must know,
Such harmonious madness
From my lips would flow
The world should listen then – as I am listening now.

To a Skylark

Percy Bysshe Shelley (1792–1822), English poet, was born at Field Place, Sussex, went to Eton and later to Oxford, but with his friend and fellow student James Hogg he was expelled for being the author of a pamphlet entitled The Necessity of Atheism. *Shelley's* Alastor *was published in 1816. In that same year he began his friendship with Byron, and about this time he wrote his* Hymn to Intellectual Beauty *and* Mont Blanc. *In 1818 Shelley left England for Italy, where he translated Plato's* Symposium *and finished* Rosalind and Helen. *In Rome, in 1819, he was stirred to indignation by the political events in England, in particular the Peterloo affair, which persuaded him to write his* Mask of Anarchy, *an indictment of Castlereagh's administration. At the end of 1819 the Shelleys moved to Pisa where he wrote some of his finest lyrics, including* Ode to the West Wind, To a Skylark *and* The Cloud. *He was drowned while sailing near Spezia, but just before his death he wrote more of his beautiful lyrics and a number of love poems inspired by Jane Williams.*

Richard Brinsley Sheridan

Mrs Candour: I'll swear her colour is natural: I have seen it come
and go.
Lady Teazle: I dare swear you have ma'am, it goes off at night,
and comes again in the morning.

The School for Scandal

The Right Honourable gentleman is indebted to his memory for
his jests, and to his imagination for his facts.

Replying to Mr Dundas in the House of Commons

Won't you come into the garden? I would like my roses to see you.

To a young woman

Richard Brinsley Sheridan (1751–1816) an Irish dramatist who settled in London, was the son of Thomas Sheridan, an actor and author. His comedy The Rivals *was written when he was only twenty-three and acted at Covent Garden in 1775. He followed this with* St Patrick's Day *and* The Duenna, *and acquired Garrick's share in Drury Lane Theatre in 1776. There he produced* A Trip to Scarborough *and* The School for Scandal, *and his famous farce* The Critic, *which appeared in 1779. He then became a Member of Parliament and held several government posts.*

Jean Christian Sibelius

Pay no attention to what the critics say. A statue has never been
erected in honour of a critic.

Jean Christian Sibelius (1865–1957) was the leading Finnish composer of his generation. His father wanted him to take up the law, but instead he studied the violin and composition at Helsingfors and went on to Berlin and Vienna. In Britain and the USA he was recognised as a major composer and became known for his orchestral En Saga *and* Karelia, *the tone poems* Finlandia *and* Night Ride *and* Sunrise, *the appealing* Valse Triste, *and seven symphonies.*

S Edith Sitwell

Still falls the Rain –
Dark as the world of man, black as our loss –
Blind as the nineteen hundred and forty nails
Upon the Cross.

The Raids 1940

Dame Edith Sitwell (1887–1964) and her brothers, Osbert and Sacheverell, were the literary offspring of an eccentric English baronet, Sir George Reresy Sitwell. Dame Edith had her own eccentricities, like dressing sometimes in medieval clothes. She set new trends in poetry by her form, including setting it to music.

Samuel Smiles

The shortest way to do many things is to do only one thing at once.

We often discover what *will* do, by finding out what will not do; and probably he who never made a mistake never made a discovery.

Self-Help

A place for everything, and everything in its place.

Thrift

Samuel Smiles (1812–1904) was born at Haddington and educated at Haddington Grammar School and Edinburgh University. He became in turn a doctor, journalist, and secretary to railway companies, but he achieved fame with his Life of George Stephenson *and the popular didactic work* Self-Help, *published in 1859.*

Logan Pearsall Smith

Thank heaven, the sun has gone in, and I don't have to go out and enjoy it.

All Trivia: Last words

There are two things to aim at in life: first, to get what you want; and, after that, to enjoy it. Only the wisest of mankind achieve the second.

Afterthoughts: Life and Human Nature

Most people sell their souls, and live with a good conscience on the proceeds.

Other People

Logan Pearsall Smith (1865–1946), born in Philadelphia, was an essayist who spent most of his life in England. He was the author of The Youth of Parnassus *(1895) and many other works, including* Songs and Sonnets *and* Milton and his Modern Critics *(1940).*

Sydney Smith

The further he went West the more convinced he felt that the Wise Men came from the East.

As the French say, there are three sexes – men, women and clergymen.

Lady Holland's 'Memoir'

I was just going to pray for you at St Paul's, but with no very lively hope of success.

H. Pearson, 'The Smith of Smiths'

I have, alas, only one illusion left, and that is the Archbishop of Canterbury.

Lady Holland's Memoir

The Reverend Sydney Smith (1771–1845), British clergyman and journalist, lived for some time in Edinburgh as tutor of Michael Hicks Beach, and became friendly with Francis, Lord Jeffrey, the Baron Brougham and Vaux, with whom he founded the Edinburgh Review *in 1802. In 1807 he published the* Letters of Peter Plymley *in defence of Catholic emancipation.*

S Edmund Spenser

Sleep after toil, port after stormy seas,
Ease after war, death after life does greatly please.

The Faerie Queene: Book 1

And all for love, and nothing for reward.

The Faerie Queene: Book 2

Edmund Spenser (1552–92) was born in London, educated at Cambridge, and then entered the service of the Earl of Leicester. In 1580 he became secretary to the Lord Deputy in Ireland and while at Kilcolman Castle completed the first three books of The Faerie Queene. *Kilcolman Castle was burnt down by rebels and Spenser and his family narrowly escaped. The last six books of* The Faerie Queene *were lost, probably destroyed in the fire at the Castle.*

Madame de Staël

Politeness is the art of selecting among one's real thoughts.

Liberty is the only thing that at all times and in every country is in one's blood. Liberty and – what cannot be separated from it – love of one's country.

Life may often seem like a long shipwreck of which the debris are friendship, glory, and love. The shores of our existence are strewn with them.

Ann Louise Germaine de Staël (1766–1817), a French author, was born in Paris, the daughter of the financier Jacques Necker, and married the Baron de Staël-Holstein in 1785. An ardent advocate of political freedom, she was banished from Paris by Napoleon, but settled at Coppet on Lake Geneva and gathered around her men like A.W. von Schlegel, Byron and Benjamin Constant. Her most influential work was De l'Allemagne, *which revealed to France the richness of German literature.*

Philip Dormer Stanhope

Be wiser than other people if you can, but do not tell them so.

Letters to his Son, 19.11.1745

Whatever is worth doing at all, is worth doing well.   **S**
Letters to his Son, 10.3.1746

An injury is much sooner forgotten than an insult.
Letters to his Son, 9.10.1746

I recommend you to take care of the minutes: for hours will take care of themselves.
Letters to his Son, 6.11.1747

Idleness is only the refuge of weak minds.
Letters to his Son, 20.7.1749

Philip Dormer Stanhope (1694–1773), fourth Earl of Chesterfield, was an opponent of Walpole and upon the latter's death became Lord Lieutenant of Ireland in 1745 and a Secretary of State in 1746. He was associated with Swift, Pope and Bolingbroke and is remembered chiefly for his Letters to his Son.

Sir Henry Morton Stanley

Doctor Livingstone, I presume?
How I found Livingstone

Sir Henry Morton Stanley (1841–1904), British explorer and journalist, was an orphan who ran away from the workhouse to ship as a cabin boy to New Orleans. Having fought on both sides in the US civil war, he became a foreign correspondent in Asia and the Middle East and was commissioned by the New York Herald *to find missionary explorer David Livingstone, missing in Africa searching for the source of the Nile. He greeted him in 1871 with this laconic remark after a journey of great difficulty. Stanley made further expeditions to Africa and became a Member of Parliament.*

Stendhal

The better you know mankind, the more you are able to overlook the little shortcomings of your friends.

Nothing is less certain than success.

S The world is full of people who can't bear being alone and to whom any remark, however uninteresting it may be, is better than nothing at all.

Heroes have intervals of fear, cowards moments of bravery, and virtuous women moments of weakness.

Stendhal (1783–1842) was the pseudonym of the French novelist Marie Henri Beyle. Born in Grenoble, he served in the ill-fated Russian campaign. Failing in his hopes of being a prefect, he lived in Italy from 1814, but suspicion of espionage drove him back to Paris, where he supported himself by literary hack-work. Balzac favourably reviewed his La Chartreuse de Parme, *and from 1830 he was a member of the consular service.*

Robert Louis Stevenson

The cruellest lies are often told in silence.

Virginibus Puerisque: El Dorado of Intercourse

There is no duty we so much underrate as the duty of being happy.

Virginibus Puerisque: An Apology for Idlers

To travel hopefully is a better thing than to arrive, and the true success is to labour.

Virginibus Puerisque: El Dorado

Here lies one who meant well, tried a little, failed much — surely that may be his epitaph, of which he need not be ashamed.

Across the Plains, A Christmas Sermon

Fifteen men on the Dead Man's Chest —
Yo-ho-ho, and a bottle of rum!
Drink and the devil had done for the rest —
Yo-ho-ho, and a bottle of rum!

Treasure Island

A child should always say what's true,
And speak when he is spoken to.
And behave mannerly at table:
At least as far as he is able.

A Child's Garden of Verses, Whole Duty of Children

Politics is perhaps the only profession for which no preparation is thought necessary.

Even if the doctor does not give you a year, even if he hesitates about a month, make one brave push and see what can be accomplished in a week.

Go, little book, and wish to all,
Flowers in the garden, meat in the hall,
A bin of wine, a spice of wit,
A house with lawns enclosing it,
A living river by the door,
A nightingale in the sycamore!

Underwoods: I. Envoy

So long as we love we serve; so long as we are loved by others, I would almost say we are indispensable.

Keep your fears to yourself but share your courage.

Robert Louis Stevenson (1850–94) entered Edinburgh University in 1867 and studied engineering, but he soon abandoned it for the law. Tuberculosis led to his frequent journeys in search of health, and his Inland Voyage *described a canoe tour in Belgium and France. His* Travels with a Donkey *followed the following year. Although very ill he contributed to many periodicals and wrote a number of essays, short stories, and fragments of travel and autobiography. He became famous because of his* Treasure Island, The Strange Case of Dr Jekyll and Mr Hyde, Kidnapped, Catriona, The Black Arrow *and* The Master of Ballantrae. *He also wrote some remarkable poetry, which was collected in* A Child's Garden of Verses *and* Underwoods. *In 1889 he went to the South Seas for the better climate and settled with his wife and stepson on Samoa.*

159

S Leopold Stokowski

It is not necessary to understand music;
It is only necessary that one enjoy it.

Leopold Stokowski (1887–1977) was an American conductor. Born in London of British and Polish parentage, he studied at the Royal College of Music and was conductor of the Cincinnati Symphony Orchestra between 1909 and 1912, and of the Philadelphia Orchestra from 1913 to 1936, becoming an American citizen in 1915. An outstanding experimentalist, he introduced much contemporary music into the United States and appeared in a number of films, including Walt Disney's Fantasia.

Jonathan Swift

And he gave it for his opinion, that whoever could make two ears of corn or two blades of grass to grow upon a spot of ground where only one grew before, would deserve better of mankind, and do more essential service to his country than the whole race of politicians put together.

Gulliver's Travels

Hail, fellow, well met,
All dirty and wet:
Find out, if you can,
Who's master, who's man.

My Lady's Lamentation

I have ever hated all nations, professions and communities, and all my love is towards individuals. . .

Letter to Pope, 29.9.1725

So, naturalists observe, a flea
Hath smaller fleas that on him prey;
And these have smaller fleas to bite 'em,

160

And so proceed *ad infinitum*.
Thus every poet, in his kind,
Is bit by him that comes behind.

On Poetry

Jonathan Swift (1667–1745), English churchman and writer, was born in Dublin and educated at Kilkenny Grammar School. A cousin of Dryden, he was admitted to the household of Sir William Temple in Moor Park near Farnham, where he acted as Secretary. While there he wrote a number of Pindarics. Returning to Ireland he was ordained in 1694, but went back to Sir William and edited his correspondence. He also wrote The Battle of the Books *and* A Tale of a Tub.

    Upon the death of Sir William, Swift went back to Ireland and was given a prebend in St Patrick's, Dublin. In 1713 he was made Dean of St Patrick's and from there he wrote the famous Drapier Letters. *In 1726 he wrote* Gulliver's Travels, *which was really a satire on parties and statesmen, but soon it became a classic of children's literature. Nearly all Jonathan Swift's writings were published anonymously and it is possible that the £200 he received for* Gulliver's Travels *was the only payment he ever had.*

Algernon Charles Swinburne

Before the beginning of years
There came to the making of man
Time with a gift of tears,
Grief with a glass that ran.
Pleasure with pain for leaven,
Summer with flowers that fell.

Atalanta in Calydon

I have put my days and dreams out of mind,
Days that are over, dreams that are done.

The Triumph of Time

S Change in a trice
The lilies and langours of virtue
For the raptures and roses of vice.

Dolores

Algernon Charles Swinburne (1837–1909) was educated at Eton and Balliol College, Oxford. In his early years he became friendly with Rossetti and his circle, but his first published volume attracted little attention. Atalanta in Calydon *had choruses which revealed Swinburne's mastery of melodious verse, and this brought him fame. In 1867 he published* A Song of Italy *and in 1871* Songs before Sunrise. *These were written during the struggle for Italian independence and showed Swinburne's political idealism.*

Tagore

God, the great giver, can open the whole universe to our gaze in the narrow space of a single lane.

Sir Rabindranath Tagore (1861–1941) was an Indian poet and a Nobel Prize-winner in 1913. His works are marked by deep religious feeling and a strong sense of the beauty of earth and sky in his native land, as well as his love of childhood. This is shown particularly in his poem The Crescent Moon. *Tagore wrote mainly in Bengali, but he also wrote in English and translated into English some of his own Indian works.*

Sir Thomas Talfourd

'Tis a little thing
To give a cup of water; yet its draught
Of cool refreshment, drain'd by fever'd lips,
May give a shock of pleasure to the frame
More exquisite than when nectarean juice
Renews the life of joy in happiest hours.

Ion

Sir Thomas Noon Talfourd (1795–1854) was a judge and author but made little impression himself. He is principally remembered as a friend of Charles Lamb, whose Letters and Memorials *he published in 1837 and 1848, although Charles Lamb died in 1834.*

Charles Maurice de Talleyrand

They have learnt nothing, and forgotten nothing.
Attributed to Talleyrand by the Chevalier de Panat, Jan 1796

It is the beginning of the end.
Remark to Napoleon after the battle of Leipzig, 18.10.1813

Black as the devil,
Hot as hell,
Pure as an angel,
Sweet as love.

Talleyrand's recipe for coffee

T War is much too serious a thing to be left to military men.

Charles Maurice de Talleyrand (1754–1838) was a French statesman. He was born in Paris and was a supporter of modern reform, but fled to the USA during the Terror of the French Revolution. He returned to France in 1796 and served as Foreign Minister under the Directory from 1778–9, continuing under Napoleon from 1799 to 1807. He represented France at the Congress of Vienna (1814–15), and was ambassador to London from 1830 to 1834.

Jack Tanner

The shop steward is a little like an egg.
If you keep him in hot water long enough, he gets hard-boiled.

Jack (Frederick John Shirley) Tanner (1889–1965), English trade unionist, was born in Whitstable. He was President of the Amalgamated Engineering Union from 1939–54, and was awarded the CBE in 1954. In 1943 he became Member of the TUC General Council, and was President from 1953–54.

Alfred, Lord Tennyson

Their's not to make reply,
Their's not to reason why,
Their's but to do or die:
Into the valley of Death
Rode the six hundred.

The Charge of the Light Brigade

'Tis better to have loved and lost
Than never to have loved at all.

In Memoriam (of Arthur Hallam)

Kind hearts are more than coronets,
And simple faith than Norman blood.

Lady Clara Vere de Vere

Knowledge comes, but wisdom lingers.

Locksley Hall

In the Spring a young man's fancy lightly turns to thoughts of love. **T**
>   *Locksley Hall*

A lie which is half a truth is ever the blackest of lies,
A lie which is all a lie may be met and fought with outright,
But a lie which is part a truth is a harder matter to fight.
>   *The Grandmother*

If thou shouldst never see my face again,
Pray for my soul. More things are wrought by prayer
Than this world dreams of. Wherefore, let thy voice
Rise like a fountain for me night and day.
>   *The Idylls of the King, The Passing of Arthur*

The mirror crack'd from side to side;
'The curse is come upon me' cried
The Lady of Shalott.
>   *The Lady of Shalott*

The gods themselves cannot recall their gifts.
>   *Tithonus*

The Lotus blooms below the barren peak:
The Lotus blows by every winding creek:
All day the wind breathes low with mellower tone:
Thro' every hollow cave and alley lone.
>   *The Song of the Lotus-Eaters*

Alfred, first Baron Tennyson (1809–92) was educated at Trinity College, Cambridge, where he became friendly with A.H. Hallam. He won the chancellor's medal for English verse in 1829 with a poem called Timbuctoo. *In 1832 Tennyson travelled with Hallam on the Continent, but Hallam died in 1833. Tennyson immediately began* In Memoriam, *expressing grief for his dead friend. This was followed by many poems and* The Idylls of the King.

William Makepeace Thackeray

There were three sailors of Bristol City
Who took a boat and went to sea.
But first with beef and captain's biscuits

T And pickled pork they loaded she.
There was gorging Jack and guzzling Jimmy,
And the youngest he was little Billee.
Now when they got as far as the Equator
They'd nothing left but one split pea.

Little Billee

Says gorging Jim to guzzling Jacky,
We have not wittles, so we must eat *we*.

Little Billee

There's little Bill as is young and tender,
We're old and tough – so let's eat *he*.

Little Billee

William Makepeace Thackeray (1811–63), English writer, was educated at Charterhouse and at Trinity College, Cambridge. He studied little, and left in June 1830 without a degree after having made friends with Edward FitzGerald, Tennyson and others. He left England and settled in Paris in order to study drawing, but in 1837 he returned to England and contributed The Yellowplush Correspondence *to* Fraser's Magazine. *He adopted the characters of George Savage Fitz-Boodle and Michael Angelo Titmarsh, and began to contribute to* Punch. Vanity Fair *appeared first in serial form, but Thackeray also lectured, his subjects being 'The English Humorists of the Eighteenth Century' and 'The Four Georges'.*

Margaret Thatcher

I've a woman's ability to stick to a job and get on with it when everyone else walks off and leaves it.

16.2.1975

Never in the history of human credit has so much been owed.

12.10.1975

If your only opportunity is to be equal, then it is not equality.

28.11.1976

Perhaps this country needs an Iron Lady.

28.3.1976

I hope to be Prime Minister one day and I do not want there to be one street in Britain I cannot go down.

1.5.1977

The lady's not for turning.

1980

Margaret Hilda Thatcher (1925–), the daughter of a grocer, became Britain's first woman Prime Minister in 1979. She was educated at Grantham High School and Somerville College, Oxford. A research chemist, she later became MP for Finchley and Parliamentary Secretary for the Ministry of Pensions and National Insurance. After being Chief Opposition Spokesman on Education and Secretary of State for Education and Science, she became Leader of the Conservative Party in 1975, and Prime Minister in May 1979. She was re-elected in 1987 for a third term.

Dylan Thomas

In the sun that is young once only,
Time let me play and be
Golden in the mercy of his means.

Fern Hill

And green and golden I was huntsman and herdsman.

Fern Hill

In the sun born over and over,
I ran my heedless ways,
My wishes raced through the house high hay,
And nothing I cared . . .

Fern Hill

The force that drives the water through the rocks
Drives my red blood.

The Force that through the Green fuse drives the Flower

Nothing grows in our garden, only washing. And babies.

Under Milk Wood

167

T *Dylan Thomas (1914–53) was born in Swansea, the son of the English master at the local school where he was educated. Beginning as a reporter on the* South Wales Evening Post, *he later became a journalist in London, and published his volume* Eighteen Poems *in 1934. He reached mastery of his medium in* Deaths and Entrances *and* Under Milk Wood, *and his short stories entitled* Portrait of the Artist as a Young Dog *are autobiographical. He died in New York while on a series of reading and lecture tours.*

James Thomson

Give a man a pipe he can smoke,
Give a man a book he can read;
And his home is bright with a calm delight,
Though the room be poor indeed.

Gifts

James Thomson (1834–82), the child of poor parents, made friends with Charles Bradlaugh, the English free-thinker and politician, wrote for the National Reformer, *and took an active part in the propoganda of free thought. His chief poem was* The City of Dreadful Night. *It was contributed to the* National Reformer *in 1874 and later re-published with other poems in 1880.*

H.D. Thoreau

I had three chairs in my house; one for solitude, two for friendship, three for society.

Walden: Visitors

The mass of men lead lives of quiet desperation.

Walden: Economy

Beware of all enterprises that require new clothes.

Walden: Economy

I never found the companion that was so companionable as solitude.

Walden: Solitude

Love your life, poor as it is. You may perhaps have some pleasant, **T**
thrilling, glorious hours, even in a poorhouse.

Walden: Conclusion

Some circumstantial evidence is very strong, as when you find a
trout in the milk.

Journal, 11.11.1854

*Henry David Thoreau (1817–62), the American writer and essayist,
was born at Concord, Massachusetts, and educated at Harvard. A
mystic, transcendentalist and natural philosopher, he rebelled against
the Puritanism of New England and the materialistic values of modern society. He built himself a cabin by Walden Pond and lived there
on practically nothing for two-and-a-half years.*

Leo Tolstoy

Happy families are all alike, but every unhappy family is unhappy in its own way.

Anna Karenina

*Count Leo Nikolaevitch Tolstoy (1828–1910) was a Russian author,
social reformer and religious mystic. He attended Kayan University,
then joined the army, but left it after the siege of Sebastopol in 1855.
Later he became a fanatical believer in non-violence. Tolstoy had
great importance and amazing power, which spread his influence far
beyond Russia and made him something of a prophet to many minds
in the West. During the last few years of his life he shared the poor life
of the peasants.*

Harry S. Truman

The White House is the finest jail in the world.

On the United States of America

It's a recession when your neighbour loses his job; it's a depression when you lose yours.

On Industry

Everybody has the right to express what he thinks. That, of course,

T let the crackpots in. But if you cannot tell a crackpot when you see one, then you ought to be taken in.

The buck stops here.

Sign on his desk

Harry S. Truman (1884–1972) was an American statesman who was President between the years 1945–1953. As Democratic Vice-President, he took the office of President on the death of Franklin D. Roosevelt, and authorised the use of the first atomic bomb on Japan which devastated the city of Hiroshima, but was instrumental in ending the war against Japan. Truman implemented the Marshall Plan to aid the recovery of post-war Europe and the 'Truman Doctrine'.

Mark Twain

The report of my death was an exaggeration.
Cable from Europe to the Associated Press

Familiarity breeds contempt — and children.
Notebooks

In Boston they ask, How much does he know? In New York, How much is he worth? In Philadelphia, Who were his parents?
What Paul Bourget thinks of us

A classic is something that everybody wants to have read and nobody wants to read.
Speeches: The Disappearance of Literature

They spell it Vinci and pronounce it Vinchy: foreigners always spell better than they pronounce.
The Innocents Abroad

Mark Twain (Samuel Langhorne Clemens, 1835–1910) first came into prominence as a writer with his Jim Smiley and his Jumping Frog. *His best-known works are* The Innocents Abroad, The Adventures of Tom Sawyer *and* The Adventures of Huckleberry Finn. *He also wrote* A Connecticut Yankee in King Arthur's Court *in 1889.*

Peter Ustinov

The sound of laughter has always seemed to me the most civilized music in the universe.

Dear Me

To be gentle, tolerant, wise and reasonable requires a goodly portion of toughness.

Peter Ustinov (1921–) is a British actor-dramatist. Born in London, he has ventured into almost every aspect of film and theatre life. He has written plays, being sometimes author, director, producer and principal actor in them. In 1963 he became joint director of the Nottingham Playhouse.

V Sir John Vanbrugh

Good manners and soft words have brought many a difficult thing to pass.

Sir John Vanbrugh (1664–1726) was an English dramatist and architect. Born in London, he designed Blenheim Palace and the first Haymarket Theatre, London.

Alfred de Vigny

Silence alone is great; all else is feebleness.

La Mort du Loup

Alfred de Vigny (1797–1863) was a French poet. Born at Loches, he joined the army at sixteen and had twelve years' service. His first volume of poems appeared in 1822 and was followed by his prose romance Cinq Mars. *His drama* Chatterton *showed his interest in England where he lived for some years, after marrying an Englishwoman in 1828.*

Publius Vergilius Maro Virgil

We cannot do all things.

Eclogues

Lucky is he who has been able to learn the causes of things.

Georgics

But meanwhile . . . time is flying that cannot be recalled.

Georgics

Even here, virtue hath her rewards, and mortality her tears; even here, the woes of man touch the heart of man.

Aeneid

Roman, be this thy care – these thine arts – to bear dominion over the nations and to impose the law of peace, to spare the humbled and to war down the proud.

Aeneid

From one piece of villainy judge them all.

V

Aeneid

A fickle and changeable thing is woman ever.

Aeneid

Do not trust the horse, Trojans. Whatever it is, I fear the Greeks even when they bring gifts.

Aeneid

I see wars, horrible wars, and the Tiber foaming with much blood.

Aeneid

Virgil (Publius Vergilius Maro, 70–19BC), the Roman poet, was born near Mantua and eulogized his own yeoman class in his poems. He was patronized by Maecenas and his Eclogues *(ten pastoral poems) appeared in 37BC. These were followed in 30BC by the* Georgics, *confirming him as the chief poet of the age. The last years of his life were spent in composing the* Aeneid, *an epic poem in twelve books intended to glorify the Julian dynasty, whose head was Augustus. An apparent forecast of the birth of Christ in the fourth* Eclogue *led to his acceptance as an 'honorary' Christian by the medieval Church and in popular legend he became a powerful magician.*

Voltaire

If God did not exist, it would be necessary to invent him.

Letters: To the Author of the Book of the Three Imposters

In this country [England] it is good to kill an admiral from time to time, to encourage the others.

Candide, In allusion to the shooting of Admiral Byng

This agglomeration which was called and which still calls itself the Holy Roman Empire was neither holy, nor Roman, nor an Empire.

I disapprove of what you say, but I will defend to the death your right to say it.

Attributed

V *Voltaire (1694–1778) was the pseudonym of the French writer François-Marie Arouet. Born in Paris, the son of a notary, he adopted his pseudonym when he had already started writing poetry while still at his Jesuit seminary. His early essay offended the authorities and during the years 1716–26 he was twice imprisoned in the Bastille and thrice exiled from the capital for having written libellous political verse. Later in life he was at the Court of Frederick the Great who had long admired him, but the association ended in deep enmity and Voltaire established himself near Geneva. He is remembered for a number of works, but particularly for* Candide *and the tragedy* Irene.

Lewis Wallace

Beauty is altogether in the eye of the beholder.

W

The Prince of India

Lewis Wallace (1827–1905) was a US general and novelist. He served in the Mexican and Civil Wars and subsequently became governor of New Mexico and minister to Turkey. He wrote the historical novels The Fair God *and* Ben-Hur.

Horace Walpole

Here lies Fred
Who was alive and is dead:
Had it been his father,
I had much rather,
Had it been his brother,
Still better than another:
Had it been his sister,
No-one would have missed her.

Had it been the whole generation,
Still better for the nation;
But since 'tis only Fred,
Who was alive and is dead
There's no more to be said.

Written after the death of Frederick, Prince of Wales in 1751

Every drop of ink in my pen ran cold.

To Montagu, 3.7.1752

Horace Walpole (1717–97), man of letters, was the fourth son of the English politician Sir Robert Walpole. He travelled to France and Italy with Thomas Gray and later he settled at Strawberry Hill, Twickenham, where he established a printing press. Here he printed Gray's two Pindaric odes and his own Anecdotes of Painting in England. *In 1764 he published his Gothic story* The Castle of Otranto, *but it is on his* Letters *that Walpole's literary reputation rests. They are said to be remarkable both for their charm and their autobiographical, social and political interest.*

175

Izaak Walton

Look to your health; if you have it, praise God, and value it next to a good conscience; for health is the second blessing that we mortals are capable of; a blessing that money cannot buy.

Compleat Angler, Part 1 Ch 21

Izaak Walton (1593–1683) was an English author born in Stafford. He settled in London as an ironmonger and wrote short biographies of his friends, Donne, Hooker, Sir Henry Wotton and George Herbert. He is well-known for his book The Compleat Angler, *the location of which was the River Lea near London.*

Isaac Watts

Let dogs delight to bark and bite,
For God hath made them so:
Let bears and lions growl and fight,
For 'tis their nature too.

But, children, you should never let
Such angry passions rise:
Your little hands were never made
To tear each other's eyes.

Divine Songs for Children, Against Quarrelling

Isaac Watts (1674–1748) was the son of a Nonconformist schoolmaster and is remembered as the author of Divine Songs for Children. *He also wrote a number of hymns, some of which have obtained a wide popularity. These include* O God, our Help in Ages Past *and* When I Survey the Wondrous Cross.

Evelyn Waugh

The great charm in argument is really finding one's own opinion, not other people's.

I do not aspire to advise my sovereign in her choice of servants.

On why he did not vote

*Evelyn Arthur St John Waugh (1903–66) was a British novelist.
Educated at Oxford, he later published studies of Edmund Campion
and Ronald Knox. His satirical and cynical novels achieved fame, particularly* The Loved One, Brideshead Revisited, *and* Scoop. *Some
of his books have been televised.*

Orson Welles

In Italy for thirty years under the Borgias they had warfare,
terror, murder, bloodshed, but they produced Michelangelo,
Leonardo da Vinci, and the Renaissance. In Switzerland,
they had brotherly love, they had five hundred years of
democracy and peace. And what did that produce? The cuckoo-
clock.
*Orson Welles added these words to the Graham Greene – Carol Reed
script of 'The Third Man')*

*Orson Welles (1915–85) was an ebullient actor-writer-producer-
director with stage and radio experience. In 1938 he panicked
the whole of America with a vivid radio version of* The War of
the Worlds, *and in 1970 he was awarded an Academy Award
for 'supreme artistry and versatility in the creation of motion pictures'.*

Duke of Wellington

I don't know what effect these men will have upon the enemy,
but, by God, they terrify me.

On a draft of troops sent to him in Spain, 1809

All the business of war, and indeed all the business of life,
is to endeavour to find out what you don't know by what you

W do; that's what I called 'guessing what was at the other side of the hill'.

Croker Papers

It has been a damned serious business – Blücher and I have lost 30,000 men.

Creevey Papers

It has been a damned nice thing – the nearest run thing you ever saw in your life . . . By God! I don't think it would have done if I had not been there.

Creevey Papers

Publish and be damned.

In reply to a blackmail letter

Arthur Wellesley (1769–1852), first Duke of Wellington, the British army commander and statesman, was born in Ireland and educated at Eton. He then entered the army and was sent to India. There he achieved victories over the Mahrattas at Assaye and Argaum, and negotiated a Peace which earned him a knighthood. After establishing his reputation in the Peninsular War he defeated the French at Vimeiro, expelled the French from Spain, and was made Duke of Wellington. Following Napoleon's escape from Elba, he defeated him at Quatre-Bras and at Waterloo. Wellington was nicknamed the Iron Duke. In later political life he was Prime Minister and Foreign Secretary.

H.G. Wells

I was thinking jest what a Rum Go everything is.

Kipps

The world may discover that all its common interests are being managed by one concern . . .

A Short History of the World

The past is but the beginning of a beginning, and all that is and has been is but the twilight of the dawn.

The Discovery of the Future

Herbert George Wells (1866–1946), English historian and novelist, **W**
was the son of a professional cricketer. He took a degree at the Royal College of Science, South Kensington, taught for some years, then made his name in science fiction with such publications as The Time Machine, The Invisible Man *and* The War of the Worlds. *Later he wrote more stories, including* Kipps, The History of Mr Polly *and* The Shape of Things to Come.

John Wesley

Do all the good you can,
By all the means you can,
In all the ways you can,
In all the places you can,
At all the times you can,
To all the people you can,
As long as ever you can.

Methodist Rule of Conduct

John Wesley (1703–91), English religious leader, was the founder of Methodism. He and his preacher brother, Charles, held many vast open air meetings, finding converts among the working class in their disillusion with formalized ritual and its lack of meaning. The two brothers published twenty-three collections of hymns as well as his collected prose Works, *and his* Journal *which is remarkable for its pathos, humour and observation of mankind. Methodism was a movement of reaction against the apathy of the Church of England that prevailed in the early part of the eighteenth century.*

Ella Wheeler Wilcox

Laugh and the world laughs with you,
Weep, and you weep alone.
For the sad old earth must borrow its mirth
But has trouble enough of its own.

Solitude

Have you heard of the terrible family They,
And the dreadful venomous things They say?

W Why, half of the gossip under the sun
If you trace it back you will find begun
In that wretched house of They.

*Ella Wheeler Wilcox (1850–1919) was an American poet and jour-
nalist. She was described as 'the most popular poet of either sex and of
any age read by thousands who never open Shakespeare'. She began
to publish poems in 1872 and her last volume,* Poems of Affection, *
was published posthumously.*

Oscar Wilde

To lose one parent, Mr Worthing, may be regarded as a misfortune; to lose both looks like carelessness.

The Importance of Being Earnest

All women become like their mothers. That is their tragedy. No
man does. That's his.

The Importance of Being Earnest

The truth is rarely pure, and never simple.

The Importance of Being Earnest

I can resist everything except temptation.

Lady Windermere's Fan

A man who knows the price of everything and the value of nothing.

Lady Windermere's Fan

I have nothing to declare except my genius.

Remark to US Customs

A little sincerity is a dangerous thing, and a great deal of it is absolutely fatal.

The Critic as Artist

I never saw a man who looked
With such a wistful eye
Upon that little tent of blue
Which prisoners call the sky.

The Ballad of Reading Gaol

Oscar Fingal O'Flahertie Wills Wilde (1854–1900), the Irish wit and dramatist, was educated at Trinity College, Dublin, and Magdalen College, Oxford. He gained a reputation as founder of an aesthetic cult. This was caricatured in Gilbert and Sullivan's comic opera Patience. *His first volume,* Poems, *was followed by several works of fiction including* The Picture of Dorian Gray. *Then came* Lady Windermere's Fan, A Woman of No Importance *and* The Importance of Being Earnest. *The most remarkable of his works are said to be* The Ballad of Reading Gaol *and* De Profundis, *both being written about his own imprisonment. His libel suit against an accusation of homosexuality resulted in evidence which led him to jail.*

John Wilmot, Earl of Rochester

Were I (who to my cost already am
One of those strange, prodigious creatures, man)
A spirit free to choose, for my own share,
What case of flesh and blood I pleased to wear,
I'd be a dog, a monkey or a bear,
Or anything but that vain animal
Who is so proud of being rational.

Homo Sapiens

John Wilmot, Earl of Rochester (1647–80), was a British poet who showed gallantry at sea in the Second Dutch War. He spent much of his time at Court where he established a reputation for debauchery. His poems include many graceful lyrics and some powerful satires, the best of which is said to be A Satire Against Mankind.

Harold Wilson

If I had the choice between smoked salmon and tinned salmon, I'd have it tinned. With vinegar.

11.11.1962

A week is a long time in politics.

1964

W One man's pay increase is another man's price increase.

11.1.1970

The monarchy is a labour-intensive industry.

13.2.1977

Sir Harold Wilson (1916–) was Leader of the British Labour Party in 1968–76, and Prime Minister in 1964–70 and 1974–76. He entered Parliament in 1945 as member for Ormskirk, and was elected for Huyton in 1950. As Prime Minister in 1964 he faced a formidable balance of payments deficit, and in 1974 found himself head of the first minority government since 1929. In an election in October 1974 he secured the narrowest overall majority in any election in recent history. Sir Harold Wilson resigned his office as Prime Minister in 1976.

Duke of Windsor

I have found it impossible to carry the heavy burden of responsibility and to discharge my duties as King as I would wish to do without the help and support of the woman I love.

Abdication broadcast, 11.12.1936

The Duke of Windsor (1894–1972), eldest son of King George V and Queen Mary, was created Prince of Wales in 1910 and served a long apprenticeship to kingship, including the navy and foreign travel. He gave up the throne as King Edward VIII soon after he inherited it because of his involvement with twice divorced American Wallis Warfield Simpson. They married and lived the rest of their lives in exile, largely in France.

William Wordsworth

I travelled among unknown men
In lands beyond the sea;
Nor, England! did I know till then
What love I bore to thee.

I Travelled among Unknown Men

I wandered lonely as a cloud
That floats on high o'er vales and hills,
When all at once I saw a crowd,

182

A host, of golden daffodils;
Beside the lake, beneath the trees,
Fluttering and dancing in the breeze.
I Wandered Lonely as a Cloud

One impulse from a vernal wood
May teach you more of man,
Of moral evil and of good,
Then all the sages can.

The Tables Turned

That best portion of a good man's life,
His little, nameless, unremembered acts
Of kindness and of love.

. . . I have learned
To look on nature, not as in the hour
Of thoughtless youth; but hearing often-times
The still, sad music of humanity.
Lines composed a few miles above Tintern Abbey

Bliss was it in that dawn to be alive,
But to be young was very heaven!
French Revolution as it appeared to Enthusiasts

We must be free or die, who speak the tongue
That Shakespeare spake; the faith and morals hold
Which Milton held.
Sonnet: It is not to be thought of

William Wordsworth (1770–1850) English poet, was educated at the grammar school at Hawkshead and St John's College, Cambridge, and left the University without distinction. In 1790 he went on a walking tour of France, the Alps and Italy. Returning to France in 1791 he spent a year there. The revolutionary movement was then at its height and impressed him greatly. He fell in love with the daughter of a French surgeon, and their story is told in Vaudracour and Julia.

The French Revolution was followed by the English declaration of war and 'The Terror', and Wordsworth's republican enthusiasm gave place to a period of pessimism. This manifested itself in his tragedy

W The Borderers *which was written in 1795/6. Wordsworth made the acquaintance of S.T. Coleridge, and a long-enduring friendship developed between them. Together they published* Lyrical Ballads *which marked a revival in English poetry. In 1843 Wordsworth succeeded Southey as poet laureate.*

Sir Henry Wotton

How happy is he born and taught
That serveth not another's will;
Whose armour is his honest thought,
And simple truth his utmost skill.

Character of a Happy Life

An ambassador is an honest man sent to lie abroad for the good of his country.

Written in a friend's album

Sir Henry Wotton (1568–1639), English diplomat and writer, became secretary to the Earl of Essex in 1595, and was employed by him in collecting foreign intelligence. He was involved in various diplomatic missions from 1604 to 1624. A collection of his poetical and other writings containing his famous work Character of a Happy Life *and* On His Mistress, the Queen of Bohemia *was published in 1651. His* Life *was written by Izaak Walton in 1670.*

Xerxes

My men have become women, and my women men.

Why Queen Artemisia's ship sank another at Salamis, 480BC

Xerxes, King of Persia (519?–465BC) was the son of Darius I. He invaded Greece and overcame the resistance of Leonidas at Thermopylae, but was defeated at Salamis in 480BC. He is the King Ahasuerus of the Book of Esther.

Y William Butler Yeats

. . . The land of faery,
Where nobody gets old and godly and grave,
Where nobody gets old and crafty and wise,
Where nobody gets old and bitter of tongue.

The Land of Heart's Desire

I have spread my dreams under your feet;
Tread softly, because you tread on my dreams.

He wishes for the Cloths of Heaven

You think it horrible that lust and rage
Should dance attention upon my old age;
They were not such a plague when I was young;
What else have I to spur me into song?

The Spur

She bid me take life easy, as the grass grows on the weirs;
But I was young and foolish, and now am full of tears.

Down by the Salley Gardens

When I play on my fiddle in Dooney
Folk dance like a wave of the sea.

The Fiddler of Dooney

William Butler Yeats (1865–1939) Irish poet and dramatist, was born in Dublin and studied at the School of Art there. He developed an interest in mystic religion and the supernatural, but at the age of twenty-one he abandoned art as a profession and took to writing, editing The Poems of William Blake, The Works of William Blake *and* The Poems of Spenser. *As a nationalist he applied himself to the creation of an Irish national theatre, and with the help of Lady Gregory and others partly achieved this ambition when his play* The Countess Cathleen *was acted in Dublin.*

Yeats' early study of Irish lore and legends resulted in Fairy and Folk Tales of the Irish Peasantry, The Celtic Twilight *and* The Secret Rose.

Under the influence of his wife and her 'communicators', Yeats wrote many works and he was awarded the Nobel Prize for Literature in 1923. He also published collections of essays and edited many books, the most important being The Oxford Book of Modern Verse *which was published in 1936. He wrote fine letters, and five major collections have been made.*

Edward Young

Tir'd Nature's sweet restorer, balmy sleep!
He, like the world, his ready visit pays
Where fortune smiles; the wretched he forsakes.

Night Thoughts

Procrastination is the thief of time.

Night Thoughts

At thirty man suspects himself a fool;
Knows it at forty, and reforms his plan;
At fifty chides his infamous delay,
Pushes his prudent purpose to resolve;
In all the magnanimity of thought
Resolves; and re-resolves; then dies the same.

Night Thoughts

Some for renown, on scraps of learning dote,
And think they grow immortal as they quote.

Love of Fame

Edward Young (1683–1765), English poet, took orders and became rector of Welwyn in 1730, where he spent the remainder of his long life, but he never received the ecclesiastical promotion to which many of his contemporaries thought him entitled.

His literary work included Busiris, *a tragedy of violence and ungoverned passion, and* The Revenge, *another tragedy, but he also published a series of satires under the title* The Universal Passion – the Love of Fame, *which were much admired. He is, however, principally remembered for* The Complaint or Night Thoughts on Life, Death and Immortality, *which became very popular immediately it was published (1742–5).*

Z Israel Zangwill

America is God's Crucible, the great Melting-Pot where all the races of Europe are melting and reforming! . . . God is making the American.

The Melting Pot, Act I

Scratch the Christian and you will find the pagan – spoiled.

The Children of the Ghetto

Israel Zangwill (1864–1926) was a Jewish writer, born in London of poor parents. He studied at London University and became famous for his Children of the Ghetto *which was written at the request of the Jewish Publication Society of America for a story depicting Jewish life among the poorer classes. He wrote novels, plays and pamphlets, made several successful lecture tours in America, and was interested in the Zionist movement.*

Emile Zola

J'accuse – I accuse.
Title of an open letter to the President of France in connection with the Dreyfus case, 13.1.1898

Emile Edouard Charles Antoine Zola (1840–1902) was a French author, born in Paris. He left school early and engaged in journalism but with little success. Showing greater aptitude for story-telling, he wrote a collection of charming tales which were published under the title Contes a' Ninon *and followed this with* L'Assommoir *which dealt with drunkenness and created a sensation. Most of his stories are very unconventional, but the exception is an idyllic tale called 'Le Rêve'.*

In 1898 he successfully took up the cause of Captain Dreyfus, a French soldier accused of selling documents of value to the German Government. Because of Zola's intervention Dreyfus was pardoned, restored to the army, and later made an officer of the Legion of Honour.

Index of Entries

Dobson, Henry Austin (1840–1921), 51–2

Donne, John (1572–1631), 52

Dostoievsky, Feodor Mikhailovitch (1821–81), 52–3

Doyle, Sir Arthur Conan (1859–1930), 53

Dryden, John (1631–1700), 53–4

Du Barry, Marie Jeanne Becu, (1743–93), 54

Edison, Thomas Alva (1847–1931), 55

Einstein, Albert (1879–1955), 55

Eliot, George (1819–80), 55–6

Eliot, Thomas Stearns (1888–1965), 56

Elizabeth I, Queen of England (1533–1603), 56–7

Everett, David (1770–1813), 57

Fields, Gracie (1898–1979), 58

Fields, W.C. (1880–1946), 58

Fitzgerald, Francis Scott (1896–1940), 58–9

Flecker, James Elroy (1884–1915), 59

Foot, Michael (1913–), 60

Ford, Henry (1863–1947), 60–1

St Francis of Assissi (1162–1226), 61

Franklin, Benjamin (1706–90), 61–2

Frost, Robert (1874–1963), 62

Gable, Clark (1901–60), 63

Gabor, Zsa Zsa (1919–), 63

Galbraith, John Kenneth (1908–), 63–4

Getty, Paul (1892–1976), 64–5

Gibran, Kahlil (1883–1931), 65

Gilbert, Sir William Schwenk (1836–1911), 65–6

Goethe, Johann Wolfgang von (1749–1832), 66–7

Goldsmith, Oliver (1728–74), 67

Goldwyn, Samuel (1882–1974), 67–8

Gorbachov, Mikhail Sergeyevich (1931–), 68–9

Grahame, Kenneth (1859–1932), 69

Gray, Thomas (1716–71), 69–70

Grenfell, Joyce (1910–79), 70–1

Grey, Sir Edward (1862–1933), 71

Guizot, François (1787–1874), 71

Gulbenkian, Nubar Sarkis (1896–1972), 71

Hall, Joseph (1574–1656), 72

Hammerstein II, Oscar (1895–1960), 72

Hardy, Thomas (1840–1928), 72–3

Harris, Joel Chandler (1848–1908), 73

Haskins, Minnie Louise (1875–1957), 73–4

Hazlitt, William (1778–1830), 74

Heath, Edward (1916–), 74–5

Hemans, Felicia Dorothea (1793–1835), 75

Henley, William Ernest (1849–1903), 75

Herrick, Robert (1591–1674), 75–6

Hindemith, Paul (1895–1963), 76

Hitchcock, Alfred (1899–1981), 76

Holmes, Oliver Wendell (1809–94), 76–7

Hood, Thomas (1799–1845), 77

Horace, Quintus Horatius Flaccus (65–8BC), 77–8

Hoyle, Sir Fred (1915–), 78

Hugo, Victor (1802–85), 78

Huxley, Thomas Henry (1825–95), 78–9

Jerome, Jerome Klapka (1859–1927), 80

Johnson, Samuel (1709–84), 80–1

Joubert, Joseph (1754–1824), 81–2

Karsh, Yousuf (1908–), 83

Keats, John (1795–1821), 83–4

Keller, Helen Adams (1880–1968), 84–5

Kennedy, John Fitzgerald (1917–63), 85

Kilmuir, Lord David (1900–67), 85–6

King, Martin Luther (1929–68), 86

Kipling, Rudyard (1865–1936), 86–7

Koestler, Arthur (1905–83), 87–8

La Bruyère, Jean de (1645–96), 89

La Rochefoucauld, François Duc de (1613–80), 89–90

Lazarus, Emma (1849–87), 90

Leacock, Stephen (1869–1944), 90

Lear, Edward (1812–88), 90–1

Lewis, Clive Staples (1898–1963), 91–2

Lincoln, Abraham (1809–65), 92–3